DEVON
CORNWALL
ODDEST
HISTORICAL
TALES

For Margherita Peretti
who began it all

First published 2021
Reprinted 2021

The History Press
97 St George's Place, Cheltenham,
Gloucestershire, GL50 3QB
www.thehistorypress.co.uk

British Library Cataloguing in Publication Data.
A catalogue record for this book is available from the British Library.

ISBN 978 0 7509 9569 6

Typesetting and origination by The History Press
Printed by TJ Books Limited, Padstow, Cornwall

DEVON AND CORNWALL'S ODDEST HISTORICAL TALES

JOHN FISHER

The History Press

YOU COULDN'T MAKE IT UP

The tales in this book are all factual. Some, but not all, are about the great and the good from Devon and Cornwall's historic past but others, by contrast, are about the small and the not so good – ordinary people with extraordinary stories – tales that have hardly seen the light of day before in a book of this kind. All of them have been chosen to interest the general reader, be they a resident or a visitor to this most historic and fascinating bottom left-hand corner of our beautiful island. Although times change and people move on, memories of their lives and the places in which they lived remain and are a joy to revisit as they are brought back to life again in this personal retelling of their unique stories.

CONTENTS

DEVON

Ship of Fools   9
Hablas Español?   11
The Spanish are Coming!   15
The Rise and Fall of Walter Raleigh   21
Devon Divided in 'A World Turned Upside-Down'   28
Will the Real Lorna Doone Please Stand Up?   33
Dirty Work at the Crossroads   37
Accidental Death of a Revenue Officer   42
King of the Gypsies – and Dog Stealer   47
The (Fairly) Glorious Revolution   52
The French Prisoners on Dartmoor   56
Napoleon's Farewell to Torbay   61
The Ladies who Lived on the Hill   69
The Lion Attack on the Exeter Coach   74
Dickens' Christmas Present to the West of England   80
The Bishop and the Slavers   84
Wife for Sale!   89
Rule Britannia!   94
The Man They Couldn't Hang   98
The Devil's Hoof-Prints   103
Lawrence of Arabia in Devon   108
How Sidmouth Inspired Betjeman   114

CORNWALL

Land of Myth and Legend	118
In at the Deep End	119
A Realm of Saints and Poets	124
The Pirate Queen of Penryn	129
The Massacre of Cornwall's Peasantry	132
Cloudesley Shovell's Horrific Shipwreck	135
A Tomb With a View	140
The Race Home From Trafalgar	145
The Lieutenant and the Toppling of the Logan Stone	149
Dolly's Ancient Tongue	154
Defoe as Travel Writer in Cornwall	157
They Called Him 'The Cornish Wonder'	162
The Queen and the Cornish Fishwife	167
A Man on Fire	172
Singing Trevithick's Praises	179
Never 'Lord Byron's Jackal'	185
'That Bloody Woman!'	187
Cornish Weather Lore	191
Sea Watching and Stargazing	204
The Unvarnished Truth About Mermaids	206

DEVON

*It wasn't all beer and skittles for West Country monks in the Middle Ages –
there was also hawking, wenching and real tennis.*

SHIP OF FOOLS

It's not surprising that with much of Devon and Cornwall bounded on
two sides by ocean, this is also England's foremost domain of seafaring
folk. It can also lay claim to being the first in England to utter the phrase
'a ship of fools', an expression now universally applied to any group that
has lost its moral compass. It began in 1508 in land-locked Ottery St
Mary and the collegiate church of St Mary on the hill above the town.

Enter one Alexander Barclay, a somewhat straight-laced Doctor of
Divinity at Oxford and now the newly appointed chaplain. What he
finds appals him. The church and its many hangers-on are in total disarray.
Here are monks and priests who, instead of going about their religious
duties, while away their days (not to mention nights) in hunting, 'hawking
at Honitone', wenching, drunkenness, gambling and – wait for it – 'the
playing of Real Tennis'. He unpacks hurriedly, reaches for his quill pen
and parchment and, closeting himself away from the hubbub, begins to
write his satirical poem 'The Ship of Fools', some of which he translates
from the original German. The poem is an allegory and a product of the
medieval conception of the Shrovetide Fool and his crew. Here is the

scholar surrounded by books but who learns nothing from them; the judge who takes bribes; the followers of fashion; the priests who fornicate or spend their time in church telling 'gestes' of Robin Hood – and so on. Although his critics say that his style is stiff and his verse uninspired, the phrase 'a ship of fools' has been usefully employed in the language ever since, but it did not make him popular in Devon. Having rubbed so many people up the wrong way, he left the county in 1513, eventually changing his religion and entering into the history books as 'Maistre Barkleye, the Blacke Monke and Poete' – a Franciscan at Canterbury. He died in Croydon on 10 June 1552.

Alas, there is no monument in Devon to the man or his epic works but if you have time to while away, you will find the woodcuts which illustrated his work online and, of course, the ageless words themselves, which remain those of a very wise man.

To be all but shipwrecked on a strange island was only the start of the tragedy for the little Spanish princess, Catherine of Aragon.

HABLAS ESPAÑOL?

Catherine of Aragon was not supposed to come up the A30 at all.

Her mother, Queen Isabella of Spain, had wanted her to land at Southampton because she had been told that it was England's safest harbour and that is where it was planned that the seriously diminutive 16-year-old Infanta was to meet up with her husband-to-be, Prince Arthur, a delicate boy more than a year her junior and half a head shorter.

But time and tide are no respecters of princes and the regal reception that awaited her in Hampshire was thrown into disarray as a great storm blew up in the Channel. This was later reckoned to be a bad omen and a forerunner of what was to follow. At 3 o'clock in the afternoon of Saturday, 7 October 1501, the future Queen of England and her entourage, all of them decidedly green and 'fearing for their lives throughout the storm', set foot on English soil for the first time, in Plymouth, where they straightaway fell on their knees on the dockside and gave thanks. Mild panic ensued as lodgings were found and the princess (who spoke only Spanish and Latin, with just a little French) was persuaded to cool her heels for a week as messengers were sent ahead, hot foot, to Winchester. For, once upon a time, wise men had told Henry Tudor that Winchester was Camelot and it was why the wily Welshman had packed his wife off to that fair city as soon as he had heard that she was pregnant – fingers crossed that there she might be safely delivered of a son and heir that he could then name Arthur. The Once and Future King. But that was fifteen years earlier.

Right now, Catherine, Arthur's bride-to-be, had reached Exeter on 19 October amid a cavalcade of escorting gentry in time for an official reception hosted and arranged by Henry VII's specially appointed event organiser, Lord Willoughby de Broke. He must have been a remarkable man and probably set up some kind of new land speed record to have covered the ground between Southampton, Winchester and Exeter to get the whole welcome back on track in such a short space of time. He found Catherine lodged at the deanery in Exeter, close by the cathedral, where the squeaky weather vane atop the church of St Mary Major had kept her awake at night until a hapless servant of the dean's was ordered aloft in the pitch dark and with a full gale blowing, to put an end to something that 'did so whistle that the princess could not sleep'.

Awaiting her party at Honiton the next day were twelve palfreys (small riding horses) for her ladies, while a litter – a covered chair mounted on poles and carried between two horses – transported Catherine herself. She objected. She was a fine horsewoman but the litter had been ordered for her by Henry himself. Thus began her progress proper, following roughly what was to become the A30, with comfort stops every 12 miles or so. Just west of Crewkerne, Somerset, she bid *adios* to the great and the good of Devon and Cornwall and *hola* to those of Somerset's dignitaries who could be mustered in time. Here was Sir Amyas Paulet from Hinton St George, and by his side Sir John Speke, a widower, from White Lackington. Whilst Paulet was well and truly married with a year-old son, Speke's 59-year-old eye, though probably dimming, was still roving, and here at the roadside on that chill October day it settled on one of Catherine's young maids of honour. She would have been about the same age as her mistress, Catherine. Her name, the records show, was Alicia or Alice (the Speke family tree spells her name Allice), and whether he courted her in English, Spanish or Latin, the old boy must have had something going for him because the following year they were married and together had one son, John, to keep the Speke line going. Fast forward 357 years to 1858 and their great (umpteenth great) grandson, John Hanning Speke was the man who discovered the source of the Nile, crossing Lake Victoria (as he himself named it) in a little collapsible boat called *The Lady Alice*.

Meanwhile, back on the Great South-West Road, Catherine's progress continued through Dorset, with overnight stops at Sherborne and Shaftesbury. She finally arrived at Dogmersfield, in Hampshire, not far from today's Fleet services. Here she took a welcome break from her journey and sent a message ahead to the rapidly approaching King Henry and groom-to-be, Arthur, telling them to hold off a while. It was, her messengers reminded the English Court, forbidden for either of them, king or prince alike, to have sight of her face before the wedding day. Catherine came from a court much influenced by Moorish Spain and would become the first veiled bride ever to be wed in the British Isles.

Nothing daunted, Henry rode roughshod over Catherine's protestations, the young couple were brought together and an impromptu party and ball were held, although history relates that the diminutive Spanish princess and her even shorter English prince did not dance together: this would have been too much of an affront to Spanish etiquette. But by this great folly, some say, the marriage was cursed, and Arthur died just five months later while they were on honeymoon at Ludlow Castle in Shropshire. When questioned on the subject many, many years later, Catherine told her inquisitors words to the effect that she had indeed been 'wedded but never bedded'.

As poor young Catherine was delivered to her destiny – and the wildly cheering crowds of London – she abandoned the litter the English had provided and chose instead to demonstrate her Spanish-ness to court and crowd alike by riding into the city on a broad-backed Murcian mule (hastily provided by the Spanish Ambassador), which she chose to ride side-saddle – and to the right – 'in the Spanish style'. She and her entourage were lodged south of the river at the area known then, as now, as Elephant & Castle, which some say is the South Londoners' corruption of the pronunciation of '*La Infanta de Castilla*'.

Yet an even greater curse than the loss of her husband was to follow, of course, when following the untimely death of Arthur she was married off to his younger brother Henry, later to become Henry VIII, and she, poor woman, the first of his six wives. Divorced. Beheaded. Died. Divorced. Beheaded. Survived. She died in 1536 aged 50, set aside for Anne Boleyn, and is buried in Peterborough Cathedral where, on the anniversary of her death each year a bouquet of yellow flowers – which some historians believe to be the colour of mourning in the Spanish Court – appears on her grave, left there by an unknown hand.

How Devon stood alone in the West as Elizabeth dithered and Spain sent its great Armada against us.

THE SPANISH ARE COMING!

It's easy to picture Queen Elizabeth I facing down the Spanish Armada in her guise as the semi-divine being promoted so skilfully by the Tudor propaganda machine and portrayed in Gower's famous depiction of her in *The Armada Portrait*. 'God blew and they were scattered!'

In reality, today's historians reveal Good Queen Bess as a serial tightwad whose miserliness and dithering brought about suffering and even death on an extraordinary scale to many of the brave men who served under her. Her sailors, at Plymouth, lived on such short rations that they were forced to fish off the sides of their ships in harbour as they awaited provisions and ammunition to fight the Armada.

She was finally persuaded to loosen her grip on her purse strings after naval commander, Lord Howard, had been forced to urge her, 'For the love of Jesus Christ, Madam, awake and see the villainous treasons around about you, against your majesty and the realm.'

One month's rations finally arrived in Devon on 23 June 1588 and were distributed to the fleet. They were told that they should make them last for six weeks. With the provisions came a warning from the queen, relates the renowned Devon-born historian James Froude, that she had forbidden further preparations to be made for supply till the month was out, after which it would take a further two weeks to assemble the rations and a further week to ship them to Devon.

The men bore their suffering without complaint but the beer that had arrived was sour and poisonous and brought dysentery, an enemy more dreaded than the Spanish, that carried them off in scores. Unable to endure the sight of this suffering, Lord Howard, the commander of the English fleet and Drake, both wealthy men, ordered wine and arrowroot for the sick at Plymouth on their own responsibility. Elizabeth later called them to sharp account for their extravagance, which had saved possibly a thousand brave men to fight for her. Drake took it on the chin. Howard refused to defend his actions and paid the bill out of his own purse.

It is late afternoon on Friday, 29 July 1588, and the first alarms are sounded out of Cornwall that the Spanish Armada is in sight off the Lizard Peninsula. Church bells ring out faint but clear across the Tamar and greenery is thrown on to blazing signal fires to create smoke and alert Plymouth, and thence the rest of England, that the invasion has come.

News of the number and disposition of the enemy ships reaches Drake and Frobisher and their fellow captains by sea the next day as a lookout ship, the *Golden Hind*, beats into Plymouth where Lord Howard's fleet awaits the news, locked in by an inclement wind and the dictates of the tide.

Plymouth's protective breakwater does not exist at this point in history. The smaller vessels – armed merchantmen for the most part – are sheltering in the mouth of the Tamar, the larger fighting ships are in the Sound, where they will stand a better chance of getting out against the tide by 'kedging'. This will involve moving a vessel forward by dropping a small anchor ahead of it and then manning winches on deck to pull the ship along.

This is a laborious process but one that will nevertheless save the day and allow Howard's men to escape and wait in the lee of Rame Head, the headland to the west of Plymouth Sound, for whatever is to come.

It is not yet dawn on the morning of Sunday, 31 July and Howard's ships now lie hidden but ready for action. If they can slip out behind the

Armada as it passes they will have the weather gauge – the windward position in relation to the enemy – answering the prayer of every English captain for the battle ahead.

First blood comes before noon. The Armada's supreme commander, Alonso Perez de Guzman, Duke of Medina Sidonia, is called to the rail of his 1,000-ton flagship, the *San Martin*, which, through the clearing sea mist, sights eighty-five English ships to windward of them. His own great bow-shaped crescent of ships known as the *lunula* formation proceeds up-Channel – transports and troopships protected in depth in the centre – warships on either side in two horns, in an unbreakable formation.

So the English are out. He ignores the entreaties of his captains to attack Plymouth and continues their progress slowly eastwards, resolved not to risk an attack on Plymouth but to follow the orders of his king and sail to the rendezvous with the Spanish army from the Netherlands he believes to be waiting to join him at Calais.

Howard has no knowledge of Spain's intentions but knows that he must harass the main central body of the Armada and prevent it from landing troops anywhere. Drake's and Hawkins's squadrons will attack the horns of the *lunula*.

Onshore, thousands have waited and watched and prayed throughout the short summer night, and as morning wears on there is a shout that sounds along the coast like a breaking wave, from Wembury to Salcombe and round to Dartmouth and beyond, as the sails of the Spanish galleons come into view.

They count them – 10, 20, 50, 130 sail. Then orange flashes and puffs of white smoke and seconds later the distant thunder of cannon fire as the galleons back their sails and slow in an attempt to entice these English into close combat. But their tormentors keep their distance, snapping at the heels of their quarry.

Like greyhounds, they bear down on the sterns of this slow-moving prey, each English vessel attempting to describe a figure-of-eight as it fires, first its long-range bow-chaser, then as it turns, a raking broadside, followed by a second as it goes about.

Devon watches the running battle unfold across the broad expanse of Lyme Bay, from Start Point to Portland Bill, attack after attack, hour upon hour. A quarter of the crews that man this English fleet are from Devon, many of them the loved ones of these townsfolk and villagers who have come to view this great drama.

Some stay to watch. Others hurry homewards and look to the safety of families, homes and belongings. Able-bodied men of the trained bands (between the ages of 16 and 60) gather up the weapons they have bought at their own expense – still longbows and pikes for the most part – and hurry to the local assembly points laid down by the Lord Lieutenant of the county, the Earl of Bath. Orders to Cornwall's and Devon's and Dorset's trained bands are the same given to all the other coastal counties. They are to march eastwards along the coast, gathering in strength as they progress, so that wherever the Spaniards choose to make landfall they can be met in numbers.

No help comes from the far west. The Cornish trained bands march only as far as the Tamar before returning to their barley harvest. Devon stands alone and the whole of Devon is in motion. Gallopers leave the crowds that gather at village squares and urge their mounts up, up to the headlands and promontories to put fresh flame to the braziers that continue to smoke the word along the coast to Beachy Head in Sussex, where, at dusk, they turn suddenly inland towards London, this time as a string of bright fires.

At sea the 29,453 men, soldiers and sailors of the Spanish Armada cross themselves as they peer through the smoke of battle upon this foreign realm, 'the great bastion of heresy' they have come to destroy. Perhaps Medina Sidonia – briefly overcoming the seasickness from which he suffers so badly – permits himself a smile at the thought of the panic he and his men must be bringing to these Western counties. For only he and his senior officers know that Devon and Cornwall are safe awhile. This great crusading force has been charged with avoiding engagements if possible and making its way up the Channel to meet up with a great fleet of barges he believes to be waiting at Calais where some 27,000 hardened Spanish troops from the occupied territory of the Netherlands will embark and cross to England with the Armada as escort.

Those troops will land between Dover and Margate, and with the Armada escorting their right flank as it sails up the Thames, will advance and put London to the flame – along with England's 'heretic and illegitimate' Protestant queen – restore Catholicism to 'this blighted realm' and crown Philip of Spain as its king.

So much for the plans of men – a plan never to unfold, thanks to the bravery of England's seamen and a great summer storm. The rest, as they say, is history.

The running battle up the Channel pauses briefly off Calais, where the Armada anchors only to discover that there is no waiting army. Fire ships are sent against them and in a desperate attempt to escape many of the galleons cut their anchor cables. For many it foreshadows the disasters that are to come.

The largest of the English attacks follows on 8 August, off Gravelines, Flanders, after which the Spanish turn on their heels and flee northwards with the English in pursuit as far as the Firth of Forth.

As they round the Shetlands in a storm and head west to follow the west coast of Ireland to home, all thoughts of invasion vanish and survival becomes paramount. Ships sink or run aground, and in the teeth of what now turns into a full-blown hurricane, unable to anchor or find shelter, twenty-four more ships founder. Their crews either drown or are slaughtered by Elizabeth's troops as they drag themselves ashore.

What Pope Sixtus V in Rome has blessed and declared Spain's Holy Crusade has turned into a disaster. England, on the other hand, dubs the storm the Protestant Wind and sees it as a sign that God supports the Reformation.

First news of the defeat reaches Spain in early September, prompting Philip to write: 'I hope that God has not permitted so much evil, for everything has been done for His service.'

Of the 130 ships sent by him against England, more than thirty-six capital ships are lost and a score and more of smaller vessels, supply ships and galleasses never return. More than 15,000 seamen and soldiers die, including those who either drown, are killed in action or later die of wounds.

Amazingly after such a tragedy, Philip strikes at England again in October 1592, with another army and a fleet of 126 ships. The orders this time are simple. Don't chance the Channel. They are to invade England via the West Country by landing in Cornwall, occupying the port of Falmouth and then marching on into Devon via Plymouth, which will simultaneously be attacked from the sea.

With most of the English fleet being refitted, Philip's cunning plan might well have succeeded – save for the October gales. This time thirty galleons are lost before they even sight the Scillies and the rest turn back.

Once more England is reminded of the inscription Elizabeth has had engraved on the Armada medals she had struck after the defeat of the first Armada: *Flavit Deus et dissipati sunt.* 'God blew and they were scattered.'

(Footnote: All dates therein are those we use in the modern calendar.)

The remarkable life, loves and tragic death of Devon's most illustrious son, his secret daughter and his loyal wife.

THE RISE AND FALL OF WALTER RALEIGH

Nobody knows for sure what became of Sir Walter Raleigh's head after he was executed.

He was publicly beheaded as a traitor in Old Palace Yard, Westminster, in 1618 and his body was laid to rest in the chancel of St Margaret's Church, Westminster, on the south side of the altar. But his devoted wife, Bess Throckmorton, took that severed head from the scaffold, wrapped it in a cloak and thence put it into a red leather, drawstring bag that she kept close by her until her own death some twenty-nine years later.

The mystery is further compounded by the fact that quite where that poor lady herself is buried is unknown. Was it put into her own coffin with her, that cherished head of Devon's most illustrious son whose life was brought to such a tragic end by a complex conspiracy of intrigue, jealousy and lies that thrived at the court of the paranoid James I? For favourite of Good Queen Bess he had been and swashbuckling braggart of a sea-dog certainly, but traitor he never was – as James well knew.

Raleigh was born at Hayes Barton in Devon in about 1553, near East Budleigh to a Protestant family – the head of which was the landed gentleman,

Walter Raleigh (a former deputy vice-admiral in the South West) and his third wife Katherine. Her sister, 'Kat', was governess to the young princess Elizabeth and remained a close friend to her in the queen's later years.

So the man who was to become Devon's most famous son, a knight of the realm, writer, poet, philosopher, soldier, adventurer (dare we say pirate?) politician, courtier – and latterly a healer – set out from his farmhouse home in deepest Devon – after completing his education at Oriel College Oxford – with some useful connections that the youthful and ambitious Raleigh was soon to exploit.

Sir Carew Raleigh, a Member of Parliament, was his elder brother, while his half-brother, Sir Humphrey Gilbert, introduced him to the royal court, where his good looks and charm made him popular – he was a legendary ladies' man – and after serving the Crown as a soldier in the French wars and then later by putting down a rebellion in Ireland, the dashing young blade became the 27-year-old favourite of the 48-year-old Queen Elizabeth, becoming captain of her personal bodyguard.

She would certainly have guessed that this tall, poetic 'softly spoken Devon lad' (he never lost his broad Devon accent, which endeared him to her) would already have sown an acre or two of wild oats during his military career but there was one particular secret he kept hidden so deeply that it only emerged in the 1970s when a will was uncovered in the archives of his Sherborne estates in Dorset.

It revealed that he left 500 marks (£332) 'To my Reputed Daughter, begotten on the body of Alice Goold, now in Ireland'. Now in Ireland? Good, Gould or Gold are all old Devon names, so was Alice a Devon lass who was later secreted away to his estates in Cork as his fame grew?

The legendary throwing down of his cloak into a puddle apart, he first attracted the attention of the queen, it is said, by taking a diamond ring and scratching words on a window pane at Greenwich Palace, where he knew she would see them.

It read, 'Fain would I climb, yet fear to fall', to which the Virgin Queen added underneath, 'If thy heart fail thee, climb not at all'. He stayed her firm favourite for ten years, could do no wrong in her eyes, took advantage of the fact and generally behaved badly to men and women of rank, making many enemies who suffered silently and bided their time waiting for his fall.

Under her wing he became 'the best-hated man in the world and she took him for a kind of oracle'. She knighted him, gave him property in England (including Sherborne Lodge in Dorset in 1592), land in Ireland, and granted him an exclusive license to import wine that was worth some £700 a year – this in an age when a wealthy merchant might live comfortably on £100. Remarkably, he was also allowed to benefit from a levy imposed on every pack of playing cards sold – which must have been an anathema to a court that did little but haunt the corridors and antechambers of the royal palaces seeking to win the queen's favour by either composing some of history's worst love poetry – or playing cards. Raleigh, by contrast, has been dubbed, quite rightly, one of the great 'silver poets' of his time.

That fall came as a result of his secret dalliance with one of the Queen's Gentlewomen of the Privy Chamber, one Bess Throckmorton (née Carew). She had come to court in 1584, aged 19. Now, aged 25, she began an affair with the now 37-year-old Raleigh and became pregnant by him.

Contemporary descriptions of her differ but are perhaps best evidenced by her portraits as being 'a tall, unusual beauty with her long face, luminous eyes, strong nose and provocatively modest lips'. Theirs was certainly a love match that endured to the grave – and beyond.

A secret marriage followed and they both returned to court after the birth of their child, Damerel, on 29 March: but there were few secrets in the Tudor court and as their marriage was exposed – by the sinister Robert Cecil – the queen became incandescent with rage for 'betraying her royal person' by marrying without her permission and had them both thrown into the Tower on 7 August, he in the Brick Tower, she elsewhere, there to remain, 'at Her Majesty's pleasure'.

He kept up a steady flow of glittering love poems to her and was released five weeks later, although an historian has written, 'Elizabeth was irritated rather than pacified by these gestures, smacking as they did of implicit defiance and a wholesale lack of remorse'. Bess, on the other hand, was kept under lock and key and only released three days before Christmas, when she learned that their child had died of the plague some time before.

Raleigh had been packed off to Dartmouth – on a mission of reprisal against the Spanish – and in the charge of a fellow Devonian, the extraordinarily wealthy and influential Sir John Hawkins – who had pleaded his case – and Bess made her way to her own family home and later to the South West, from where they were expected to plead for forgiveness. When neither of them did, Raleigh was nevertheless taken back into the fold.

Two more children were born to Walter and Bess: Walter at Lillington in Dorset and Carew at Sherborne.

His daring-do and exploits beyond the court – in which he was trapped and found stifling – are, of course, all the stuff of British history. Raleigh the seafarer, the explorer who masterminded and financed the colonising expeditions to North America – naming Virginia in his monarch's honour. He was the scourge of the Spanish Main and made himself and people around him, but especially his queen, wealthy with plundered treasure.

Although both tobacco and potatoes were already known from Spanish explorers, Raleigh popularised them, introducing the potato to Ireland – first to his own estates there – and actually promoted tobacco as a good cure for coughs.

Raleigh designed and built his own warship, which he named the *Ark Raleigh* but later gave it to the queen, who renamed it the *Ark Royal*. It became the flagship of the English fleet against the Spanish Armada. He was the queen's naval adviser and with Hawkins improved the design of the ships that were so successful against the Spanish.

Even monarchs sometimes know which side their bread is buttered and Elizabeth's anger abated, as she consented to his idea of pursuing his long-held dream of discovering the fabled golden land of El Dorado, which he believed to be in Guiana, now Venezuela. Although the mission was unsuccessful, it did not put an end to his dream, which he attempted to fulfil one final time by playing it as a 'Get-out-of-jail-free card' with Elizabeth's successor, James.

At Elizabeth's death in 1603, Raleigh fell foul of the ex-king of Scotland and was again imprisoned in the Tower, this time under the trumped up charge that he had been involved in a Catholic plot to unthrone James. There he tended a small herb garden, was granted an exercise walk along part of the battlements, concocted 'cordials' and healing balms of many kinds (he regularly prescribed for Ann of Denmark herself, the wife of the king) and writing.

His philosophical writings and poetry are all still in print and wonderful to read. Most famous of all perhaps is his *Historie of the World*, first taking the reader through Biblical times and grinding to a halt in AD 168. But there he drew the line, writing 'for whosoever in writing a modern history shall follow truth too near the heels, it may haply strike out his teeth'.

In 1616 he was pardoned and allowed to form a second expedition to find the elusive city of El Dorado on his oath that he would attack neither Spanish ships nor colonies, there having now been a peace treaty signed between the two countries. That 1617 expedition was to prove a disaster.

No gold was found and while Raleigh was elsewhere, his close friend and captain (and one-time fellow prisoner in the Tower with him) Lawrence Kemys, attacked and burned a Spanish settlement. Raleigh's eldest son, Walter, just 22, was shot and killed in that same action.

Hearing the news, Raleigh told Kemys, 'You have undone me', Kemys replying simply, 'I know then, Sir, what course to take'. He returned to his own cabin and shot himself. Raleigh returned, empty handed, was arrested, tried and sentenced to death to appease Spain.

He was now an old man, broken by ill health and imprisonment, and wrote these lines in his final night in the Tower. 'I cannot write much, God he knows how hardly I steale time while others sleep, and it is also time that I should separate my thoughts from the world.' And then, 'Even Such is Time':

> Even such is time, that takes in trust, Our youth, our joys, our all we have, And pays us but with age and dust; Who, in the dark and silent grave, When we have wandered all our ways, Shuts up the story of our days. But from this earth, this grave, this dust, My God shall raise me up, I trust.

In his final note to Bess he wrote, 'Begg my dead body which living was denied thee; and either lay it at Sherburne or in Exeter Church, by my Father and Mother; I can say no more, time and death call me away.'

He was beheaded outside the Palace of Westminster early on the bitterly cold morning of 29 October 1618. From the scaffold he told the crowd: 'I have lived a sinful life, in all sinful callings; for I have been a soldier, a captain, a sea-captain, and a courtier, which are all places of wickedness and vice.'

Then he asked the executioner to hurry because it was cold and he did not want his enemies to think that he trembled for fear. 'Make haste,' he said, 'for I have a long journey ahead of me.' It took two strokes of the axe to sever his head and when it was held aloft at the executioner's customary cry of 'Behold the head of a traitor' it was met with silence from the crowd save for a lone voice that cried out, 'We have not such another head to be cut off!'

In preparing this chapter, the Carew family historian Sir Rivers Carew was consulted on the subject of the mystery surrounding the burials of both Sir Walter and Bess Throckmorton (née Carew). He wrote that Bess had wanted her husband's body to be buried at her brother's church of St Mary the Virgin, Beddington, in Surrey.

Sir Rivers spoke of the author and historian Ronald Michell, who speculates 'that Raleigh's body may actually have been buried at Beddington after all'. 'He based this on the letter she wrote to 'My best brother Sir Nicholas Carew at Beddington' asking him to allow this, saying, 'The Lords have given me his ded boddi' and 'This nit hee shall be brought you with two or three of my men'.

Sir Rivers said: 'Michell argued that Sir Nicholas would hardly have refused his sister's appeal, and that this is what actually happened. In her letter she also expressed her wish to be buried there; I don't know if she was.'

The mystery remains but it may explain why Raleigh's youngest son, Carew Raleigh, who was 'killed' in London in 1680 (how and why is not known) was first buried in St Margaret's Church, Westminster 'with his father' but then later reburied at Beddington. Was his father's head entrusted to him on his mother's death in 1647 and eventually placed in his own coffin at his own death? And is Bess also buried there so that all of them might be together at last?

Perhaps we shall never know for certain. The last word on that particular subject therefore is with Ann Smith, the archivist at Sherborne Castle in Dorset, who wrote: 'The ghost of Sir Walter is reputed to walk the grounds of Sherborne Castle on 29 October, but I must say I have never seen him in all the years I have worked here (nor met anyone who has). If ever I do, I hope I have the presence of mind to ask him some searching questions!'

But looking for an alternative and more fitting ending to Raleigh's life should properly lie with his biographer, William Stebbing, who concluded his authoritative work on Devon's most illustrious son by writing:

> Yet, with all the shortcomings, no figure, no life gathers up in itself more completely the whole spirit of an epoch; none more firmly enchains admiration for invincible individuality or ends by winning a more personal tenderness and affection.

Trust in God and keep your powder dry!' (Oliver Cromwell).
'Who shall govern this realm, King or Parliament?' (Charles I).

DEVON DIVIDED IN 'A WORLD TURNED UPSIDE-DOWN'

For some of us, the English Civil War has never ended: today's splendid re-enactment societies such as The Sealed Knot, for example, attract huge crowds throughout the summer months as they continue to play out the bloody battles and skirmishes that once split our nation in two.

If so much of our contemporary story-telling is to be believed, the flamboyant long-haired 'Cavaliers' are most often portrayed as the good guys, while the kill-joy close-cropped 'Roundheads' take the role of the not so good. But both names were coined by the protagonists themselves to insult each other, so more properly we were all of us in those days either Royalists or Parliamentarians, whether we liked it or not.

King Charles 'lost', of course, both the war and his head, and Oliver Cromwell 'won' but it was only for a few short years (1642–51). With the Restoration of the Monarchy – and the reintroduction of general merriment and bonhomie – revenge was swift. Cromwell's corpse – three years in its grave – was first dug up, then strung up before finally having its head put on a spike outside Westminster Hall where it remained until 1685.

So which side was Devon on? The answer is not a simple one. Seventeenth-century Devon country folk were, for the most part, poor and uneducated and were told by their landlords which side they were to support and ultimately to fight for. By contrast, there are many instances within the ranks of the more well-to-do where one son was sent to fight for the king, the other for Parliament: hedging one's bets is nothing new.

In simple terms, most of Devon could have done without it but all of Devon found itself embroiled in the dark struggles of what turned out to be three English Civil Wars that claimed the lives of more than 85,000 in armed conflicts and 100,000 more from war-related diseases: this from a population of some 5 million.

It is a matter of record that a young shepherd and his flock who inadvertently strayed into the preparations for a battle in 1644 – a full two years into the conflict – had to have it explained to him that the king and Parliament were at war. 'Whassat?' enquired the good swain, 'As them two fallen out then?'

North Devon was the first part of the county to feel the effects of the war, with bloody skirmishes and sieges at Ilfracombe and Barnstaple, but there is hardly a community of any size, town or village in Devon that does not have its tales of confrontation and hardship. Cromwell, in charge of the New Model Army's cavalry, and General Sir Thomas Fairfax, its supreme commander, came into Ottery St Mary in east Devon, took over the town and stabled their horses inside the church. The town's great house, Chanters, was their base and in its dining room there is a panel recording:

> In this room Oliver Cromwell in the fall of the year 1645 convened the people of the town and neighbourhood and demanded of them men and money for the Civil War. Here also on October 29th Members of Parliament on behalf of both houses presented Sir Thomas Fairfax with a fair jewel and hung it about his neck in honour of his skill and valour at Naseby fight.

Meanwhile, outside, one of Cromwell's bored cavalrymen whiled away the afternoon by taking pot shots at the remarkable weather vane that once topped the parish church. Called the 'Trumpeting Cock' by the long-suffering people of the town, it was hollow and fitted with a two-note whistle that 'crowed' in the wind.

Naseby had been decisive in the fortunes of the king. He lost most of his veteran infantry and officers, all of his artillery and stores. But worse still, in the captured baggage train Fairfax's troops found his personal papers revealing his attempts to draw Irish Catholics and foreign mercenaries into the war. As the war raged to and fro across England and with towns and villages often changing allegiances depending on the arrival of the latest occupying force, Charles's queen, Henrietta Maria, heavily pregnant with her ninth child, left the Royalists' capital of Oxford and fled to the West Country, intending to escape to France from Falmouth – Plymouth having already declared for Parliament.

She got as far as Exeter, a city then in Royalist hands following siege upon siege, arriving on 1 May 1644, and stayed at Bedford House, close to the city centre, where, aged 35, on 16 June 1644, she gave birth to Princess Henrietta Anne. At this time, the Parliamentary forces led by the Earl of Essex were yet again threatening the west and planned to attack Exeter and hold the queen to ransom as a bargaining chip in the king's surrender. Although she had had a difficult labour and the baby was poorly, the poor woman hurried on again, this time to Cornwall and thence to France, leaving her new baby in the care of Lady Dalkeith, who saw to it that the sickly infant was baptised in 'the new font' in the cathedral on 21 July 1644.

King Charles and his army arrived in Exeter and saw his still-surviving baby daughter for the first and only time on 26 July 1644. He then moved quickly into Cornwall, where he defeated the Parliamentary forces of the Earl of Essex at Lostwithiel. But the war continued to ebb and flow as the opposing forces battled for supremacy in the west until Parliament gradually gained the upper hand. While Royalist Exeter was still under siege, this time by Fairfax and Cromwell, 10,000 Parliamentarians broke away from the siege and marched north to Torrington, where the Royalists had barricaded the town – and as fate would have it – had stored eighty barrels of gunpowder in the church.

The battle began in pouring rain and total darkness on the bitterly cold night of 16 February 1646; It was to be the last battle in the west. As

Fairfax waited for dawn to break, Cromwell arrived with his cavalry and advanced on the barricades at the edge of the town to test their strengths by firing blindly into them. All hell broke loose.

Some 17,000 men and horses fought in the freezing downpour, street by street, with the terrified townsfolk watching the bloodshed below them from upstairs windows. After the exchange of fire there was little time or space to reload, as pikemen rushed against pikemen and musket butts were used as clubs in the hand-to-hand fighting along the narrow streets and alleyways until, by some mischance and nobody knows how, the powder stacked in the church exploded. It took the roof off the building and killed more than 200 men from both sides.

The Royalists scattered towards Cornwall: it was the beginning of the end of resistance by their forces in the west and led eventually to the capture and execution of the king. Dartmouth and Exeter surrendered to the New Model Army in April 1646. One of Fairfax's first actions in the city was to issue an order whereby the young Princess Henrietta Anne, now aged 3, was given written safe conduct to travel to London together with the loyal Lady Dalkeith and her small household. Once out of sight of their escort at the Devon border however, the good lady headed for Dover and then to France, where she reunited the little girl with her mother. Did Fairfax connive at this deviation from the route? Lord Thomas Fairfax, or 'Black Tom' as he was known to both sides, was an honourable man on and off the battlefield. He opposed the execution of the king and as a consequence was pardoned by Charles II at the Restoration while many, many others were not.

Which brings events to a fateful conclusion with the Restoration of the Monarchy. On 30 January 1661, the twelfth anniversary of the execution of Charles I, the remains of the body of the Lord Protector of England, Scotland and Ireland was exhumed from its crypt and subjected to a posthumous execution. At least that is what the Royalists thought they had done. Cromwell's body had been buried in Westminster Abbey, amid great pomp and ceremony, alongside the body of his daughter, Elizabeth, who had died earlier and her tomb remained undisturbed. But was it really Cromwell's body? It is thought by some that his family, friends and followers who could see what was coming had already removed the corpse and reburied it several times to cheat the vengeful Royalists of their grisly goal.

Cambridgeshire, London, Northamptonshire and Yorkshire are all places that have been suggested – while that head itself, when it was finally lifted from its spike outside Westminster Hall, finished up beneath the floor of the antechapel at Sidney Sussex College, Cambridge – warts and all. But whose head?

With the status quo restored, the vacated Cromwell vault in Westminster Abbey was later used as a burial place for eleven of Charles II's twelve illegitimate descendants; his illegitimate son, the would-be revolutionary the Duke of Monmouth is buried – minus his head – beneath the chapel floor in the Tower of London, having been beheaded publicly for treason on 15 July 1685. His head was displayed on a spike, not outside Westminster this time, but on London Bridge.

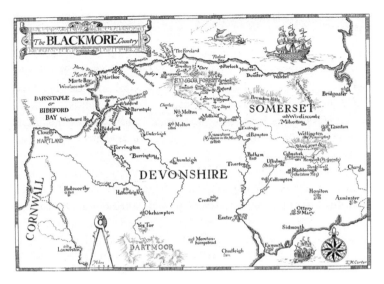

John Ridd, the man Lorna marries, tells her story in his old age. She had long black hair, dark eyes and was beautiful, he said. For the rest she embodies unblemished purity of the Victorian-era romantic heroine.

WILL THE REAL LORNA DOONE PLEASE STAND UP?

The Doones got away with murder, quite literally. For although Blackmore's classic nineteenth-century novel *Lorna Doone*, set on the Devon and Somerset borders, is a work of fiction, it is so cleverly researched and interwoven with historic fact that even the good people of Exmoor nowadays sometimes find it difficult to distinguish between the two, while the Exmoor tourist industry – understandably – seldom tries.

Exmoor owes Lorna plenty. First the book and its countless reprints, then no fewer than ten films and television serialisations over the years, all conspire to pull in the visitors. In short, Lorna continues to do for tourism in the West Country what the rich harvest brought about from those Poldarkian biceps in the barley do for Cornwall.

The name Doone is real enough but the Lorna part was a fiction. Nowadays a popular first name, it did not exist until it was coined for his heroine by her creator, Richard Doddridge Blackmore, in 1869 – in the same way that J.M. Barrie conjured up the name Wendy out of thin air in 1904, as a consort for Peter Pan. The real Doone family lived on Exmoor in the seventeenth century right enough, and were a thoroughly bad lot. Murder, kidnapping, plunder, arson, cattle rustling, burglary and highway robbery were all in a day's work for the bloody-handed villains of this extended family, who seemed to have led charmed lives, untouched by the law in their hidden valley that straddled the border of the two counties.

The authorities in Devon probably claimed that it was the responsibility of their neighbours in Somerset to raise the funds and organise the armed force that was needed to penetrate their rural stronghold and flush them out, and vice versa. In his novel, Blackmore suggests that it was all due to bribery and corruption, and that the Doones had the authorities eating out of their hands. Who knows the truth of it 400 years after the events?

Blackmore's father was a country parson and Richard went to Blundell's School in Tiverton, Devon, and thence to Exeter College, Oxford. After university he married and worked first as a lawyer, then a market gardener and finally as a schoolmaster. He read an article on the Doones in a magazine while on holiday in north Devon and was inspired to write the book. He wrote thirteen novels in total, with varying success but *Lorna Doone*, which passed into more than forty editions in his lifetime, put him in the front rank of Victorian writers, although it is probably fair to say that Lorna and her sweetheart, John, stand out as the only truly memorable creations of their author. Except for the fact that Blackmore took seventy-five chapters to unfold this historic tale of romance and swashbuckling adventure, the plot is essentially the classic boy (John Ridd) meets girl (Lorna Doone), boy loses girl, boy gets girl. John Ridd's father had been murdered during a Doone rustling raid at the start of the book and Lorna (we are given to believe) is the granddaughter of Sir Ensor Doone, the ringleader of the red-handed clan. An impossible match and irreconcilable differences you would think? Read on. It gets worse.

Lorna's cousin, Carver Doone – what a name for the blackest villain ever painted in English literature – is vowed to wed her when Ensor dies and he becomes chieftain. Poor Lorna. John and Lorna meet when he climbs a waterfall that turns out to be a back way into the Doone kingdom, where he spies on Lorna and becomes instantly and totally enamoured. Seventy chapters and 350-odd pages later they....

but enough! Who would dare spoil the ending of what is a thoroughly gripping, bodice-ripping yarn by a fine writer and good storyteller.

Once part of the Scottish nobility, the real Doones were exiled by the Earl of Murray from lands they claimed were theirs in about 1620. The leader of this émigré pack, Sir Ensor Doone, who had murdered his twin brother so that he might lay claim to Doune Castle – still up there, near Stirling (they used it at the start of *Monty Python and the Holy Grail*). The entire brood trundled into Devon via London, with all the portable possessions they could lay hands on. Here, they tried to charm fellow Scot king James to their cause, to no avail. Given short shrift by the canny king, Ensor was sent packing with the Jacobean equivalent of 'go West ye villain' ringing in his ears, and so set out upon his weary way until he stumbled across a countryside much like the one from which they had been thrown out. But this time, to what must have been Ensor's undoubted joy, it was inhabited by gentle, rural folk who could be dominated by the gang with ease and set upon and robbed at knife point. Here then were the good people of wild and wonderful Exmoor and here they decided to stay. Unchecked by neighbours, who did what they could to keep out of their way, local women were coerced into the fold and other followers and hangers-on joined them, whence they bred like flies to become what Ensor called his 'great and loyal family' and to the rest of the West Country, a lawless gang.

The valley they took for their own is still there and very much a part of the tourist trail. It runs north to south from tiny Malmesbury at its head – below County Gate on Exmoor – down through to Badgeworthy (where John Ridd's father was murdered on the way home from Porlock). This is the heart of *Lorna-Doone*-the-book country. Here is the water slide, so-called 'Lorna's Cott' and nearby Oare House and Oare Church (where Blackmore's grandfather was once rector), where the dastardly Carver shot poor Lorna on her wedding day. Blackmore took his inspiration for that particular climactic event from an actual shooting at St Michael's Church at Chagford, Devon. There is a plaque there that tells how one Mary Whiddon, may she rest in peace, was shot dead by a jealous suitor on her wedding day, 11 October 1641. Was our Lorna killed? We are honour bound not to divulge any more of the book. All we said was that Lorna was shot. Full stop.

What better way to close, therefore, than with the words of the man who loved her. And this perhaps is where fact and fiction marry, for although the words are those of John Ridd – now an old man – they come from the pen of Blackmore, a man who, it is known, was devoted to his wife Lucy. Blackmore surely drew upon his feelings for her when he finished his book with this, very telling last paragraph:

> Of Lorna, of my lifelong darling, of my more and more loved wife, I will not talk; for it is not seemly that a man should exalt his pride. Year by year her beauty grows, with the growth of goodness, kindness, and true happiness – above all with loving. For change, she makes a joke of this, and plays with it, and laughs at it; and then, when my slow nature marvels, back she comes to the earnest thing. And if I wish to pay her out for something very dreadful – as may happen once or twice, when we become too gladsome – I bring her to forgotten sadness, and to me for cure of it, by the two words 'Lorna Doone.'

There was a time when virtually every main crossroad in the West was marked either by a witch's grave, a suicide's burial or a gibbet.

DIRTY WORK AT THE CROSSROADS

The last women to be hanged for witchcraft in Britain were from Devon. Three of them died at Heavitree, on the outskirts of Exeter, by having ropes with slip knots tied around their necks. Then they were lifted bodily off the ground. It was how they did things in those days and at that place. It was August 1682 and thousands of people walked out from the city on the Honiton road, following behind the hapless trio and up the hill to where the road still forks to watch the spectacle and listen to any final words from the women before cheering wildly as they left the ground to kick their legs in the 'gallows dance'. The three unfortunates were Temperance Lloyd, Mary Trembles and Susanna Edwards, three poor, terrified women who were brought down from Bideford to Exeter to one of the two 'official' places where Devon's death penalties were carried out. One of them, Temperance Lloyd, and the only one to have made any kind of 'confession', was probably mentally deranged. The other two screamed their innocence until the end.

At Tyburn in London, where the vast crowds demanded a better view of events, those convicted met their ends by being pushed from the tailboard of a cart (the same cart that had brought them from prison, seated on their coffins), their nooses already tied to the crossbeam of the gallows. For charity's sake they were given a last stiff drink before their final journey began – 'one for the road'. That was their last, for now they were decidedly 'on the wagon'. At the Tyburn tree, as the cart was whipped away friends or family might rush forward and hang on to the legs of their loved ones to cut short their agony. Not so in Devon. At Heavitree, a place like many others in England that takes its name from the terrible tree that once served as a gallows there, death was a much more drawn out affair. What mattered on these occasions was that justice was seen to be done by those who administered the laws of the day and witchcraft was only one of the crimes that called for the death penalty. Others included murder, treason, highway robbery, sheep stealing, cattle rustling, forgery, arson, house-breaking, thievery, assault and rape. There was one exception to hanging for murder. Women who murdered their husbands were never hanged. Instead they were put to death by being burned alive. Their crime was known as 'petty treason' and defined under the Treason Act of 1351. It was seen as 'an assault on the majesty of the State' as well as the actual victim and therefore 'against the natural order of things'. The Act was repealed in 1825 but the last woman to be burned alive in Exeter was Rebecca Downing, a servant girl who died on 29 June 1782 for poisoning her mistress.

For reasons best known to themselves, the authorities in Devon decreed that these public burnings should happen not at Heavitree but at Southernhay, just outside the city walls, on a piece of scrub land used periodically for an annual fair. Perhaps it was so that the administering clergy did not have so far to walk from the cathedral in inclement weather? It was there on 15 November 1557 that Agnes Prest was chained to a post and burned alive, not for murder but for denying the Catholic doctrine of transubstantiation. As with all burnings, the ashes were scattered about the place afterwards so that come Judgement Day there will be no bones to rise from the grave with the chance of a life to come. On the same spot in 1571 one Agnes Jones was burnt to death for poisoning her husband. There were doubtless many other burnings here on this spot, on the west side of Southernhay, nowadays a select, tree-lined commercial area and marked on a 1709 map as 'The Burning Place'.

But Devon's crossroads were always the preferred places to hang people, especially highwaymen and footpads, because bodies would be left swinging, in a gibbet, for as long as the magistrate decided. This not only acted as a deterrent to other miscreants, it also served to reassure travellers that they were in a law-abiding part of the realm. Bodies in gibbets – body-hugging iron cages – could stay there as long as twenty years, and they were designed in such a way that the corpse remained visible, held together for as long as possible after decay set in. Sometimes criminals were put in these gibbets alive and simply left to die. The most famous 'criminal and traitor' to be thus despatched was Robert Welsh, the Catholic vicar of St Thomas's in Exeter, who was placed in a gibbet alive (by the then Protestant council of Exeter), before being hauled to the top of his own church tower in Cowick Street for 'preaching against the new religion' (Protestantism) during the Prayer Book Rebellion of 1549. A contemporary account records how:

> [He was] hung in chains, having on his priest's vestments, with a holy bucket, a sprinkling brush, a small bell, a pair of beads, and other Romish articles hung about him; where he remained for a long time. He made little or no confession, but took his death very patiently; and had certainly proved a very useful member of the commonwealth, had not his follies and vices over-balanced his virtues.

It took him four days and nights to die but his body was left on the gibbet until 1553, when it was 'safe' for Catholics once more. This was during the brief reign of Queen Mary I, *aka* Bloody Mary, for her burning alive of many hundreds of Protestants, men, women and children.

Little wonder that hundreds of years later so many of these places of execution still have disturbing tales attached to them. These intersections, it was thought, also served to confuse the spirits of those who had committed dark deeds. Rather than move on to judgement, they lurked (and perhaps continue to lurk, some say) in this no man's land, beyond the limits of a town and between human habitations. It is why suicides were also buried at crossroads. The problem was that following the Murder Act of 1751 many Devon crossroads became little more than bone yards as corpses rotted in the gibbets that were now commonplace. For in their enlightenment, the lawmakers, having abolished the practice of hanging drawing and quartering, needed a tougher law to deter murderers and the proliferation of gibbeting was the perceived answer. Parliament's new law 'for better preventing the horrid crime of murder' stated that 'in no case whatsoever shall the body of a murderer be suffered to be buried'. The Act mandated either public dissection or the 'hanging in chains' (so-called gibbeting) of the cadaver. Sometimes both. On occasion, these gibbets were erected not at a crossroad but close to the scene of the crime itself – Samuel Pepys, commenting in his diary, expressed disgust at the practice where the sight and smell of decaying corpses was offensive and 'pestilential' and so a threat to public health. A contemporary visitor to England, the forerunner of French travel writers, Cesar de Saussure, wrote:

> After hanging murderers are punished in a particular fashion. They are first hung on the common gibbet, their bodies are then covered with tallow and fat substances, over this is placed a tarred shirt fastened down with iron bands, and the bodies are hung with chains to the gibbet, which is erected on the spot, or as near as possible to the place, where the crime was committed, and there it hangs till it falls to dust. This is what is called in this country to be hanged in chains.

It was not only criminals who were denied a Christian burial. The best-documented burial of a Devon suicide at what were then crossroads is that of 'Kitty' Jay and dates from the late 1700s. The discovery of the grave is first documented in the *North Devon Journal*, 23 January 1851:

> In the parish of Manaton, near Widdecombe on the moor while some men in the employ of James Bryant, Esq., of Prospect, at his seat, Hedge Barton, were removing some accumulations of way soil, a few days since, they discovered what appeared to be a grave. On further investigation, they found the skeleton of a body, which proved from enquiry to be the remains of Ann Jay, a woman who hanged herself some three generations since in a barn at a place called Forder, and was buried at Four Cross Lane, according to the custom of that enlightened age.

From Torquay's Gallows Gate to Gibbet Hill near Brentor or Hangman's Stone in East Devon, the county abounds with places where the name is a giveaway to the ghoulish goings-on that once went on there. Many more are not obvious at all but are still probably 'spooked' – thanks to the man given the job of punishing the rebels following the Monmouth Rebellion in the west in 1685 – the monster, Judge Jeffreys. After the capture and execution of the ringleader, the Duke of Monmouth, who had landed at Lyme Regis, many hundreds of ordinary Devon and Dorset peasants were rounded up, 'tried' and executed. This began by hanging and then by disembowelling, after which the heads and quarters were dipped in pitch and salt and displayed on poles, gibbets and roadside trees. These body parts were placed nearest to the hamlets and villages from whence the rebels had come – as a warning to anyone else contemplating treason. Those parts stayed there for years, nobody daring to take them down.

So there you have it. Not only does Devon have more miles of road than any other county in England, it also has more tales of headless horses, headless horsemen and headless coachmen roaming in the gloaming than you might care to shake a chain at. But before you start checking and rechecking your rear-view mirror when the days become dimpsey and nights draw in, it may be a comfort to ponder the suggestion that many of these apparitions may not be what they seem. There is good reason to believe that many of them were dreamt up by eighteenth-century smugglers to spread fear and alarm among the good people of the county. There was (and still is, come to that) nothing better than the thought of a close encounter with a headless horror to keep a body's head firmly under the duvet when 'the gentlemen' and their five and twenty ponies go trotting through the dark.

Post mortem: Judge Jeffreys went on to become Lord Chancellor of England and was buried in a vault directly under the altar table of St Mary's Church, Aldermanbury, in the City of London, two pennies on his closed eyelids, his hands crossed solemnly across his chest, there to patiently await his resurrection. Alas, alack for the poor judge, those expectations were to be dashed by Adolph Hitler, no less. Came 1940 and the Blitz, and the church received a direct hit from a Nazi bomb and all traces of Jeffreys vanished. Dust to dust? Perhaps, but that is not quite the end of the story. The stones of the church were duly gathered up, numbered and transported to Fulton, Missouri, in 1966 and reassembled in the grounds of Westminster College, as a memorial to Winston Churchill who had made a memorable 'Iron Curtain' speech there in 1946.

Murder excluded, there were 139 crimes you could hang for in Georgian England – but smuggling wasn't one of them.

ACCIDENTAL DEATH OF A REVENUE OFFICER

Caught red-handed, smugglers were either fined or imprisoned but this didn't prevent the worst of them from murdering any poor Revenue officer who stood in their way. With any luck, a jury could be made up of the accused's neighbours, while the magistrate assigned to the case was more than likely a customer and quite possibly one of the players in the smuggling network itself.

In the seventeenth and particularly in the eighteenth and nineteenth centuries, European wars kept import duties high on tea, wines and spirits, laces and tobacco: smuggling therefore became a lucrative means of income for many, a tempting sideline for half-starved fisherfolk and not so half-starved farmers and other landowners along the coast, to whom it became a way of life over generations.

Just about every family in East and South Devon – not to mention Cornwall or Dorset – would have had some knowledge of where to source the things they needed from this black market or had friends or a family member 'in the trade' itself. Every coastal village, every lane and footpath had its lookouts; many cottages, farms, barns and parsonages their hidey holes.

Once out of sight of land, some Devon fishermen would stow away their nets and head out across the Channel (Cherbourg and Roscoff were the most-favoured ports of call), bringing back everything Rudyard Kipling's famous poem 'A Smuggler's Song' catalogues:

> Five and twenty ponies, Trotting through the dark – Brandy for the Parson, 'Baccy for the Clerk; Laces for a lady, letters for a spy, And watch the wall, my darling, while the Gentlemen go by!

But especially favoured was French brandy in handy 2 and 4 gallon kegs. Once landed, these were roped together and thrown over the backs of men or ponies waiting to lift their illicit cargoes off the beaches by dead of night. If danger threatened, the barrels could instead be lowered over the side, just out of reach of low tide, when heavily weighted nets were used to sink the 'catch'; at other times heavy anchors kept lines of kegs hidden. The location of the contraband was marked with corks and recovered – when the coast was clear – by men in rowing boats using grappling hooks. This practice, which continued well into the 1850s, was called 'sowing the crop'. Waiting the arrival of the smugglers on shore were farmers, who kept long trains of donkeys and mules to move the barrels and bales from their hiding places along the shoreline and carry them quickly inland. The pretence for keeping these droves of pack animals was that they were used exclusively for bringing up bags of kelp and sea sand from the beaches to dress the land.

Hardest to convince of these claims were 'the preventative men', or 'picaroons' to use the derogatory nickname given them by the smugglers. Among seafaring men, 'picaroon' was a term of low abuse meaning rogue or villain. These much-maligned men were the forerunners of the Customs and Excise service (nowadays the UK Border Force) and were actively employed on land and sea to check the trade. Much of popular literature and later Hollywood portrays these Revenue men as the spoilsports in the drama, while the exploits of the smugglers themselves, often led by a super-suave swashbuckler, are highly romanticised. Unlike piracy, smuggling was not a capital offence, yet many a good Revenue man lost his life 'by accident' in pursuance of his duty, while there are accounts of others who were kidnapped and tortured to death by the gangs of heavies or 'batmen', who smugglers employed as guards to do their dirty work for them.

Blackest of these was the villainous Hawkhurst gang, which operated along the south coast and as far west as Dorset and Devon. Their bloody careers climaxed in 1747 when 'for sport' they seized a preventative officer, an elderly man, one William Galley, whom they buried alive in a foxhole. His travelling companion, Daniel Chater, a shoemaker by trade, was a witness in a forthcoming smuggling trial and had been under Galley's protection and actually sharing a horse at the time they were attacked. This poor unfortunate they kept chained in a shed and tortured with knives over several days before finally putting him out of his misery by throwing him down a well and pounding him to death with rocks. So much for the romance of smuggling.

Fourteen perpetrators of that particular wickedness were eventually brought to justice. Not so those who threw another 'picaroon' off a Devon cliff one dark summer's night long ago. Dark because smugglers preferred the darkest nights in the lunar calendar to make their runs. Thus, the riding officers who patrolled the lonely shorelines of South and East Devon knew exactly when trouble was brewing. The smugglers waited for the darkest nights and the highest tides: nights when the wind blew from the south or south-west were most favoured. This enabled the smugglers to sail straight into the cove or inlet chosen for the drop without the need to tack. To tack meant to zig-zag towards a destination and this made the smugglers vulnerable to interception by one of the patrol vessels operated by the Revenue out of Plymouth, fast and well-armed cutters. (Before firing, the cutter was bound to hoist its Revenue colours – both pennant and ensign – no matter whether day or night).

Many were armed with 'smashers', the deadliest weapon in Nelson's navy: short-range carronades mounted in the bows. They fired a massive 68lb cannon ball, a single hit from which would turn a smuggler's fishing boat into matchwood or punch a hole through both sides of a well-armed French privateer. The mere appearance of one of these vessels on the horizon, therefore, was often sufficient for contraband to be quickly jettisoned, while most privateers wisely preferred to turn on their heels and try their luck another night: and luck was what smugglers needed most – along with a clear sighting of the two signal fires that would be lit by their cronies on shore to enable them to steer safely between them and as far up the beach as their momentum allowed.

The night of 9 August 1755 was perfect for the trade: black as pitch, a high tide, a steady, on-shore breeze and a 1-day-old moon. The only fly in the smugglers' ointment that night was John Hurley. Hurley was a riding officer, 45 years old, married with children and lived in a cottage in the village of Branscombe. It would not be hard to imagine his wife's final words of caution to him as he saddled his horse and rode out into the darkness of that fateful night. It was the last time she was to see him alive. His battered and broken body was later brought back to her in a cart with the tale of 'a terrible accident' having occurred. John Hurley's burial place is in St Winifred's churchyard, Branscombe, and if you read between the lines of his epitaph chiselled into the side of his tomb – and still just about legible – you too may conclude that he was murdered. Or is it an epitaph? It reads more like a warning to anyone else sticking their noses into other people's business. This is what it says:

Here lieth the body of Mr. John Hurley, Custom House Officer, of this place. As he was endeavouring to extinguish some fire made between Beer and Seaton as a signal to a smuggling boat then off at sea, he fell by some means or other from the Top of the Cliff to the bottom, by which he was unfortunately killed. This unhappy accident happened on the 9th of August in the year of our Lord 1755 Aetatis Suae (age) 45. He was a brave and diligent Officer, and very inoffensive in his life and conversation.

Precisely how many other revenue men were murdered by smugglers in Devon in the eighteenth and nineteenth centuries we will never know. The names and service records of many of this gallant band of men were destroyed in a fire at the Customs House.

No talk of Devon's smugglers would be complete without mention of the notorious – not to say colourful – Jack Rattenbury (1788–1844), the self-styled Rob Roy of the West, although 'Devon's-own Harry Houdini' might be nearer the mark if you ever get to plough through his richly embroidered memoirs, ghost-written for him by a local clergyman, John Smith, pastor of the Unitarian Congregational Church in Colyton.

Rattenbury was born in Beer in the very year that the black market for contraband was given a sudden and dramatic boost as Great Britain declared war on France – this time for siding with the American revolutionaries. To support his poor mother, Jack's amanuensis relates how he seems to have spent most of his days – along with many of his nights – hauling contraband along the south Devon and Dorset coast and trying, without much success at times, to keep one jump ahead of the Revenue as he pursued 'the trade' the hard way. Twice press-ganged by the Royal Navy, once in Plymouth and once in Lyme Regis, he somehow manged to his getaway both times. He was also captured three times by the Revenue in mid-smuggle but twice escaped, like a will o' the wisp – the third time by walking out of the magistrate's court scot free when the case against him failed to hold water. Or should that read brandy? Back-door brandy backhanders were perks for beaks in Georgian England.

Rattenbury relates how he once escaped the clutches of French privateers and made an even more astonishing getaway when as a prisoner of the Revenue he climbed over the side of the cutter and hid among the petticoats of a group of 'wives and sweethearts' who had rowed out to see their menfolk before they were hauled off to face trial and imprisonment. Lucky Jack indeed.

As he grew older, and bent on reform he said, he married and tried to settle down and open a pub. Twice he went back to his old ways, but with times becoming increasingly hard for an old smuggler past his prime and the pickings getting smaller, the cliff paths steeper with every birthday, and the pub failing for good measure, in one final attempt to turn an honest shilling he became, for a brief while, a contractor supplying blue lias lime that was used in the construction of the little harbour at Sidmouth. 'Alas, poor Jack, his story finally ended in 1836 when so little had he profited by his free-trading expeditions, that he was fain to accept a pension from Lord Rolle of a shilling a week. So it can be said of Devon's most famous smuggler that he died an honest man.'

Which quotation, taken from the notebook of a Victorian gentleman writing of the end of the trade in Devon in the 1850s or thereabouts, might have been the end of Jack too, save for the good people of Beer themselves. To this day they celebrate Jack Rattenbury Day each year in the village where he was born, and drink to his memory – no doubt in what else but the finest French brandy, available (during opening hours) from any good licensed grocer or pub in the west of England – duty paid.

Bamfylde · Moore Carew.
King of the Beggars.

You couldn't make it up – or did he make it up?

KING OF THE GYPSIES – AND DOG STEALER

Bamfylde-Moore Carew, the man with the unlikeliest of first names, was born in Bickleigh, Devon, in 1693 and died in Tiverton in 1759. That much is for certain: more or less.

As for the rest, you may read his life story 'in his own words' in *The Surprising Adventures of Bamfylde-Moore Carew, King of the Gypsies – and Dog Stealer*, in which he confesses to pursuing a career as an out-and-out rogue, a premier league confidence trickster, an unscrupulous charlatan, mountebank, a blind (and sometimes lame) beggar, a practised dog stealer, an accomplished pickpocket, a master of disguises and, lest we forget, King of the Gypsies.

He was born one July morn at Bickleigh, near Tiverton, where many bearing the ancient and honourable name of Carew lie buried and his father, Theodore Carew, was the vicar. He was named in honour of his two godfathers, the Honourable Colonel Hugh Bampfylde and one Major Moore. Aged 12, he was sent to Tiverton School and fell in with a gang of classmates who kept a formidable pack of deerhounds. Came the day they skipped lessons and flattened a farmer's cornfield in pursuit of a deer and Carew decided to make a run for it rather than return to school to face the beating or his home to face a sermon. He vanished for a year and a half until Carew judged it safe to return to Bickleigh, having finished his 'education' in the interim among a band of Gypsies. His book boasts that he had been a quick study and he had majored in most of the tricks of the trade by his return. The bad penny had turned up once more, this time having gone from bad to worse. He did not stay long.

He immediately set about taking up a number of disguises and defrauding friends and neighbours out of money and was again forced to take to the road – this time to avoid arrest. In Georgian England there were genuine Gypsies and then there were also gangs of professional vagabond-thieves who pretended to be what they called Egyptian Gypsies. In this guise the gangs hawked goods, practised phoney fortune telling, tricking gullible serving girls into letting them into rich houses where they could make off with the silver and mingled with crowds at fairs to pick pockets, as well as the usual thefts from farmyards, chicken runs, market stalls and homesteads, as they ploughed their wicked ways across the land.

Was he a rogue or did he make most of it up simply to sell books? Two hundred and fifty years later the jury is still out, trying to separate fact from fancy, but read Henry Fielding's *Adventures of Tom Jones* (a classic work of fiction from 1749) and you will find a chapter devoted to hero Tom's encounter with Carew and company in a wood, where he is most decidedly ensconced as the King of the Gypsies. That chapter adds nothing to the *Tom Jones* plot. Strange, unless perhaps Fielding, a West Country man and a lawyer and magistrate as well as an author, is simply taking the opportunity to add to the authenticity of his own yarn by recording an actual encounter he himself had with the villainous Carew?

Meanwhile, back at our own tale, we need tell that our hero was also a good actor and could feign madness at the drop of a hat. For in Georgian England, when and where it was customary to transport a man (or woman or child) for stealing so much as a loaf of bread, exceptions were made and leniency shown to those who were clearly mentally challenged. These itinerants were simply turned out on to the highway again and pointed firmly in the direction of the next parish. Still one jump ahead of the law, his chosen road led him to sign on to a ship bound for Newfoundland. On his return he landed at Newcastle, where he posed as the ship's mate, charmed an apothecary's daughter into eloping with him and headed back to the South West. Together they led the nomadic life and he re-joined the band of rogues that had taken him in earlier. They gravitated – along with most of the rest of England's Gypsy fraternities – to the rich pickings to be had at London's Bartholomew's Fair. Here, as fate would have it, the old Gypsy King Clause Patch died, and Carew – who by now not only held their first-class honours degree in flim-flammery, but was also versed in Latin and Greek – was voted King of the Gypsies.

But uneasy lies the head that wears the crown, for within a few months he was back in Devon, caught, imprisoned, convicted as an idle vagrant and sentenced, at Rougemont Castle, Exeter, to be taken to Bideford to be transported to Maryland. (Most Devon ports did a good trade in those days importing tobacco and exporting convicts.) As he tells it, he managed to escape immediately on his arrival at the quayside in America as the planters were casting an eye over the latest arrivals. He made it into the woods but was quickly recaptured, whipped and had an iron ring fastened round his neck. A second escape brought him to a village of friendly Native Americans who, rather than turn him in to claim their reward must have fallen under his charms because, he tells us, they set him free. He then made for Pennsylvania, swam the Delaware River and eventually reached Boston Harbour via Philadelphia and New York – in an assortment of disguises, including that of a Quaker.

Here he signed up on a British man-of-war, homeward bound. On his arrival at Bristol, he escaped the clutches of re-enlistment (or indeed imprisonment) by having first pricked his hands and face with the point of a dagger and rubbing in a mixture of salt and gunpowder – one of the many tricks in his repertoire – to feign smallpox. He then set about tracing his wife (and daughter), he said, but leaving them in Bath, found himself in Scotland (1745) where he joined forces with – wait for it - Bonnie Prince Charlie himself, accompanying him to Carlisle and Derby. Well, well. But when things got tough for the Young Pretender, as well as our young pretender, Carew suddenly became both lame and insane and limped back to the South West, where he pursued a long and profitable career. He disguised himself variously as a Presbyterian preacher, a shipwrecked sailor, a ruined farmer, a penniless widow (he often told fortunes disguised as an old woman), a rat catcher, and a woman whose daughter had been killed in a fire. 'Mad Tom' and countless other characters were all portrayed to bring on tears, making it all the easier to extract money from the good people of Devon.

All went well until one day, on a visit with his wife and daughter to Exeter – where they were 'visiting friends' – he found himself, alone, taking the air along the front at Topsham, doubtless thinking what he might steal or whom he might dupe when suddenly his Gypsy luck ran out. Quicker than one might cry, 'Grab that villain!', he was recognised by a merchant called Davey who had been defrauded by him. As ill luck would have it, an ancient mariner named Captain Simmonds was at that very moment about to shove off for a sea voyage and, being an opportunist, he had Carew bound and bundled into the bottom of his boat and rowed out to the good ship *Phillory*, then at anchor off Powderham Castle, waiting for a fair wind. Here the hapless Carew, now known throughout the West Country as 'King Gypsy', was added to its cargo of prisoners bound for transportation to the Colonies. Eleven weeks later he found himself once more back in Maryland.

This time he escaped in a canoe, slipping off unnoticed during the convict sales. He travelled by night, stealing food from empty homes in the day. He crossed the Delaware again, this time on the back of a stolen horse, making a bridle with his handkerchief. (All escaping convicts at the end of eleven-week-long sea voyages carried very, very long handkerchiefs with them for just such a purpose.) Back in Boston, he was able to secure his passage back to England.

Fast forward through the mists of time and Carew's yarn spinning came to the ears of the good Sir Thomas Carew of Haccombe, Devon, a distant relative, who offered to provide for him if he would only give up his wicked wandering ways. Apparently he refused the offer but then had a change of heart 'after winning a fortune in a lottery'. Amazing. It certainly sounds as though the old Gypsy luck had returned – and what a wonderful way to finish the last chapter of 'his' book. He bought a house in Bickleigh and settled down. His daughter made a good marriage and he had grandchildren, His final years were spent 'idly' in retirement, writing his books. The first of them was first published in 1745, with the contents 'noted by himself during his passage to America'. Although Carew 'the author' almost certainly poured out a stream of 'facts', the author was more likely to have been one Robert Goadby, a printer in Sherborne, Dorset, who published the book. But if that is the case, it is much more likely that Carew first dictated it to what we would nowadays call a 'ghost writer' – in this instance the literate and enterprising Mrs Goadby, one who not only knew which side her bread was buttered but was also well qualified to know what made a best seller when she wrote one.

Bampfylde-Moore Carew outlived his wife and died on 27 August 1759. He is buried in Bickleigh churchyard, where may he rest in peace. The last word on the subject of our story is best left, perhaps, to an equally worldly wise author, Henry Fielding, the man who met the 'King of the Gypsies' and also wrote so vividly of fate and fortune and morals in Georgian England. 'A rich man without charity is a rogue: and perhaps it would be no difficult matter to prove that he is also a fool.'

There is nothing new about 'spin', as the good folk of the West Country discovered in 1688.

THE (FAIRLY) GLORIOUS REVOLUTION

Forget 1588 and the failure of the Spanish Armada: when Prince William of Orange led the Dutch invasion of Britain 100 years later, he managed to pull the whole thing off successfully without a shot being fired, made himself king and founded a dynasty. It all started, as far as the common people of this island were concerned, on 5 November 1688 in sleepy old Brixham, Devon. The startled fisherfolk of the county stood open mouthed – not to say awestruck – at the stage management that went into first the landing and then the calculated, showy progression through the muddy highways and by-ways of the rain-soaked and decidedly soggy West Country, first to Exeter and thence on to London.

The 38-year-old Dutch prince and his party dropped anchor with fifty-three warships bristling with cannon, followed by hundreds of transport ships carrying an army of 20,000 men and 7,000 horses, along with ten fire ships – quite enough muscle to stop a war before it could even get started – which was precisely the idea. For this was what some historians tend to brush over as 'The Glorious Revolution' but which was really a carefully orchestrated *coup d'état* and several years in the planning, to get rid of the Catholic James II (younger son of Charles I) and his heirs from the throne and replace them with a Protestant king. It would also give the Dutch an ally against the French – but that is another story.

On Tuesday, 6 November, William's army advanced to Newton Abbot, where the honeyed words of his declaration of intent were solemnly read to the people. He lodged at Ford, the ancient seat of Sir William Courtenay, who managed not to be at home lest he should compromise himself before he could see which way the wind might blow. Meanwhile, off stage, the massive job of unloading the prince's D-Day landing continued. Exeter 'surrendered' on 9 November and William climbed up into the pulpit in the cathedral and redelivered his message of peace and love to the great and the good of the West Country; but not before he made his entry into the city 'with great pomp', according to historian Thomas Macauley:

> Such a sight had never been seen in Devonshire. Many went forth half a day's journey to meet the champion of their religion. All the neighbouring villages poured forth their inhabitants. A great crowd, consisting chiefly of young peasants, brandishing their weapons, had assembled on the top of Holdron [sic] Hill, whence the army marching from Chudleigh first descried the rich valley of the Esk [sic], and the two massive towers rising from the cloud of smoke which overhung the capital of the West. The houses were gaily decorated; doors, windows, balconies, and roofs were thronged with gazers and the people of Devonshire were overwhelmed with delight and awe. Descriptions of the martial pageant were circulated all over the kingdom.
>
> First rode Macclesfield, at the head of two hundred gentlemen, mostly of English blood, glittering in helmets and cuirasses, and mounted on Flemish war-horses. Each was attended by a negro, brought from the sugar plantations on the coast of Guiana. The citizens of Exeter, who had never seen so many specimens of the African race, gazed with wonder on the black faces, set off by embroidered turbans and white feathers. Then with drawn broadswords came a squadron of Swedish horsemen in black armour

and fur cloaks. They were regarded with strange interest; for it was rumoured that they themselves had slain the huge bears whose skins they wore. Next, surrounded by a goodly company of gentlemen and pages, was borne aloft the prince's banner. But the acclamations redoubled when, attended by forty running footmen, the Prince himself appeared, armed on back and breast, wearing a white plume, and mounted on a white charger.

Then as now, the good people of the west of England were genuinely pleased to see new faces in such vast numbers and were quick to seize the opportunity to improve their lot. 'The country people brought all sorts of provisions in abundance because it yielded them money and went off well. It was when an ancient woman[...] broke from the crowd, rushed through the drawn swords and [prancing] horses, touched the hand of the deliverer, and cried out that now she was happy.' Macauley says that he smiled.

So, what of this smiling conqueror himself? He was no oil painting, according to his sister-in-law, who wrote that she thought him 'the ugliest man in Europe', while a contemporary chronicler, one Gilbert Burnet, is only a little more flattering:

He had a thin and weak body, was brown haired, and of a clear and delicate constitution: he had a Roman eagle nose, bright and sparkling eyes, a large front, and a countenance composed to gravity and authority; he was always asthmatical and the dregs of the smallpox falling on his lungs, he had a constant deep cough. His behaviour was solemn and serious, seldom cheerful, and but with a few: he spoke little and very slowly, and most commonly with a disgusting dryness, which was his character at all times, except in a day of battle; for then he was all fire, though without passion.

The bad weather continued and the 'roads' got steadily worse, to a point where local oxen were recruited to drag the guns and ammunition through the quagmire churned up by the advancing cavalry. So vast an army was hard to move and infantry often found it easier to abandon the track and trudge the adjoining fields. Thus William's great host became strung out over 20–30 miles as it was forced to head 'up country' in stages and sometimes along three more or less parallel routes. First stop, according to the army chaplain in the Dutch force – an English cleric given the role of diarist of the invasion – was 'St. Mary Otterie'. As that advanced section moved on next day to Axminster, so the second section left from Exeter to 'Otterie' and so on. Fanned out through the mud, their advance struggled by leaps and faltering bounds via Beaminster, Crewkerne and Lyme and then on to Sherborne.

Gilbert Burnet picks up his pen once more to deliver the coup de grace to his tale by telling us that James, meanwhile, having gathered his army at Salisbury, addressed the crowd in the town's market place:

> Telling them he would open his blood for the Protestant Religion (whereas he had been seen at Mass all the morning by many of his Auditors who whereupon derided him in their Hearts). No sooner had he ended his speech, but immediately falls to bleeding of his Nostrils very violently and his blood could not be stopped [in] any manner of way.

The rest is history, the mercifully short version of which is that he fled to London. James met William's envoys on 1 December and was offered humiliating conditions and subsequently 'allowed to escape' and seek refuge in France. William of Orange and his wife were crowned as William III and Mary II on 11 April 1690. Eight months later the historic Bill of Rights was passed, confirming them as monarchs and the exclusion of Catholics from the throne. Finally, in July 1690, 'King Billy' defeated James at the Battle of the Boyne.

James returned to Paris, where he lived as 'an austere penitent' until his death of a brain haemorrhage in 1701 at the age of 67. In the interim, Britain had accepted what had been a *coup d'état* and bought what the Dutch spin doctors promoted as a peaceful regime change. The so-called Glorious Revolution 'in defence of ancient freedoms' had been sold, lock stock and barrel, and Britain prospered in many ways as a consequence: and has seldom looked back.

A purpose-built granite prison in the middle of nowhere, but a heaven on earth for the men marched out from the rotting prison hulks in Plymouth Sound.

THE FRENCH PRISONERS ON DARTMOOR

Thousands of captured Frenchmen were imprisoned in Devon during the Napoleonic wars which, off and on, ran between 1803 and 1815. Many hundreds of them died there during their incarceration and are buried in mass graves at Dartmoor Prison. So too are 271 American sailors captured during the War of 1812 with America.

Initially they were put into military prisons and prison 'hulks', derelict ships anchored in estuaries. Conditions on these hulks were appalling, with overcrowding, poor diet, crude sanitation and little in the way of exercise or fresh air. Many of these hulks were in Plymouth and too close for comfort to Plymouth Docks and the temptation for hundreds of highly qualified young *marins* to break out and 'liberate' one or two of His Majesty's men-of-war in a getaway. Death rates rose to an unacceptable level and it was decided to build an escape-proof prison on land. The Plymouth hulks were emptied one at a time and the local militia escorted the prisoners and their possessions as they were marched out of the city and up onto the moor. The prison that awaited them, then as now, was a forbidding-looking place: grey and cheerless, it had been built from Dartmoor granite by local labour in the middle of nowhere and as far as could be judged on that late May afternoon in 1809 as the first contingent arrived, it also looked escape-proof. But to those ragged, pale-faced men escaping those sodden, cheerless, wooden hellholes that had contained some of them for years, it must have looked like a paradise. In describing Dartmoor's rolling hills and valleys at that time, a Monsieur Jules Poulain, a Frenchman who is said to have lived at Princetown to be near a friend who was confined there, wrote, 'Think of the ocean waves changed into granite during a tempestuous storm, and you will then form an idea of what Dartmoor is like.'

Dartmoor Prison was the brainchild of a man called Thomas Tyrwhitt, a well-connected, well-heeled Old Etonian, Oxford graduate and son of an Essex vicar. Mr Tyrwhitt (later to receive a knighthood) seems to have done rather well out of the deal. It was helped by the fact that he was secretary to the Prince of Wales on the Duchy Estates and shared with him his dream of turning Dartmoor into a prosperous place. This would simply involve draining all the bogs, clearing away all those tiresome rocks and boulders so that thousands of acres of golden corn might be planted and the moor transformed to become 'the bread basket of the West Country'. Tyrwhitt's other crackpot schemes included laying iron tracks across the wildly undulating terrain from Dartmoor to Plymouth so that horses could pull his wagons loaded with granite to the docks. Tyrwhitt's own Herne Hole quarry supplied all of the cut stone for the construction of the prison and he was also granted the licence to hold a market and a fair at his creation of Prince's Town (later to become Princetown). Here prisoners could trade their rations, handicrafts, clothes and other personal possessions for money. The money was then used to gamble or to buy vegetables from the locals, who flocked to the town on market days.

The building as then constructed cost £130,000, and is described in the architect's notes thus:

> The outer wall encloses a circle of about 30 acres – within this is another wall which encloses the area in which the Prison stands – this area is a smaller circle with a segment cut off. The prisons are five large rectangular buildings each capable of containing more than

1,500 men; they have each two floors, where is arranged a double tier of Hammocks slung on cast-iron pillars, and a third floor in the roof, which is used as a promenade in wet weather. There are besides two other spacious buildings, one of which is a large hospital, and the other is appropriated to the Petty Officers. The entrance is on the western side, the gateway, built of solid blocks of granite.

No sooner had they settled in than the French began to organise. They conducted their own courts, and devised their own punishments for misdemeanours. Most remarkably of all perhaps, the French prisoners in the UK formed no fewer than twenty-six lodges and chapters of Freemasons in England and elsewhere. The one in the neighbourhood of Dartmoor was at Ashburton, and the only evidence of it is an undated certificate granted to one Paul Carcenac, described as assistant commissary, the lodge being described as Des Amis Reunis (the Reunited Friends). Many of the prisoners of war were allowed out on parole:

> upon condition that he gives his parole of honour not to withdraw one mile from the boundaries prescribed there without leave: that he will behave himself decently and with due regard to the laws of the Kingdom, and also that he will not directly or indirectly hold any correspondence with France during his continuance in England.

The Devon towns set aside for prisoners on parole were Ashburton, Okehampton, Moretonhampstead and Tavistock, whilst periodically French officers were also billeted at Tiverton. The behaviour of 150 who lived there was described in an official report as 'exemplary' but then added, 'Some of them have made overtures of marriage to women in the neighbourhood which the magistrates have very properly taken pains to discourage'. One thinks perhaps of the Second World War and the impact some American servicemen had on some communities, who described them as being 'over-sexed, over-paid and over here'. There must have been many a Devon lass who fell under the Gallic charms of their lodgers. Printed warnings came not a moment too soon and were pasted up across the moor for the benefit of anyone who could read, while church pulpits were used to reinforce the message and remind all parties of the rules of engagement:

NOTICE IS HEREBY GIVEN

That all such prisoners are permitted to walk or ride on the Great
Turnpike Road within the distance of one mile from the extreme
parts of the Town (not beyond the bounds of the Parish) and that
if they shall exceed such limits or go into any field or cross road
they may be taken up and sent to prison and a reward of 10 shillings
(50 pence) will be paid for apprehending them. And further that such
prisoners are to be in their lodgings by 5 o'clock in the winter and
8 o'clock in the summer months.

Each prisoner was assigned a residence and received a fixed sum for
his maintenance. He was allowed to engage in any kind of business or
occupation. Many taught languages or carved trinkets, chess pieces or
model ships from animal bone. At the Devon Summer Assize 1812,
Richard Tapper, described as of Moretonhampstead, carrier, Thomas
Vinnacombe and William Vinnacombe (his brother) of Cheriton Bishop,
described in the indictments as smugglers, were indicted and convicted
for aiding and assisting with 'divers other persons unknown', the escape
of the following men: Casimer Baudouin, an officer in the French Navy;
Allain Michel and Louis Hamel, captains of merchant vessels; Pierre
Joseph Dennis, a second captain of a privateer; and Andrew Fleuriot, a
midshipman of the French Navy, to escape from Moretonhampstead.
The five Frenchmen paid £25 down, and then £150 on the day they
broke their parole and made a dash for the sea and freedom. They were
taken on horseback down from Moretonhampstead, suitably disguised,
to Topsham on the estuary below Exeter, and placed in a large boat,
described as 18ft long. Alas, with five escapees, and the three smugglers
on board, they ran into trouble not far from Exmouth, when and where
the boat grounded on the bar and they were spotted and rounded up.
The Frenchmen were returned to Dartmoor, the 'smugglers' to prison
in Exeter.

Dartmoor had been filled to capacity in less than a year after its
completion. Matters became worse with the arrival of American
prisoners (allies of the French) in April 1813, and outbreaks of diseases
– pneumonia, typhoid and smallpox – became widespread. In total

about 6,500 American sailors were imprisoned at Dartmoor, mostly naval prisoners, and impressed American seamen discharged from British vessels: about 1,000 of them were black. Both the French and the American wars finished in 1815 and repatriations began, but before that came to pass there was what has been dubbed a massacre of seven American prisoners (and some sixty seriously wounded) when guards opened fire at a crowd of prisoners they believed (mistakenly) to be on the point of 'causing an affray'.

The prison then remained empty until 1850, when it was rebuilt as a convict gaol for the most hardened criminals, who were sentenced to long terms of hard labour. When the prison farm was being established in about 1852, all the prisoners' remains were exhumed and reinterred in two cemeteries behind the prison. There they still lie, more than 11,000 Frenchmen and 271 Americans. Their epitaph reads: *Dulce et decorum est pro patria mori*, a line from Horace's Odes that can be translated as, 'It is sweet and proper to die for the fatherland'.

Wilfred Owen used the line in his similarly titled poem, '*Dulce et Decorum Est*', it is now often referred to as 'The Old Lie'.

When Napoleon exited the field at Waterloo, few could have guessed that within a few short weeks he would be sleeping aboard a British warship off Torbay.

NAPOLEON'S FAREWELL TO TORBAY

Napoleon always had a plan and after the Battle of Waterloo, on Sunday, 18 June 1815, it was that he should beat a retreat to America – a country sympathetic to the French cause since their own Revolution of 1776 – to live to fight another day.

So, barely one jump ahead of the approaching Allied armies, he headed to Paris, where he told the provisional government that he had decided to abdicate as emperor – again. He had done it once before of course, in 1814 when the Allies besieged Paris and had him imprisoned on Elba. Oh, and one more thing, he told them. He would need two frigates put at his disposal at Rochefort, on the west coast of France, for himself and his entourage, together with American passports for all of them. This was the end game. If he stayed in France, where many were demanding an end to the bloodshed across Europe and a return of the Bourbons, there would be a civil war, which would not go well for him. This time the Allies would surely lock him up and throw away the key.

The remote island of St Helena in the South Atlantic had been mooted, but first they would have to catch him. And waiting to do just that was Frederick Maitland, captain of HMS *Bellerophon*, the seventy-four-gun lead ship of the blockading force patrolling near Brest. Bonaparte knew that getting out and on to the high seas was going to be no easy matter. He was also fearful that the French crew of the frigate would mutiny and hand him in – or worse still kill him outright. He therefore sent emissaries out to the *Bellerophon* to stall for time whilst he put another plan into operation. The letter they carried – dictated by him – said, 'The Emperor is so anxious to spare the further effusion of human blood, that he will proceed to America in any way the British Government chooses to sanction, either in a French ship of war, a vessel armed en flute, a merchant vessel, or even in a British ship of war.'

Maitland had already been ordered not to let Napoleon escape and to conduct him to the nearest anchorage in England – which was Torbay. He stood his ground and extended the invitation for Napoleon and his party to come aboard under safe conduct, whence they would be taken to England. Meanwhile, a message arrived from a British agent further along the coast that revealed the degree of Napoleon's desperation at this time. Maitland later wrote:

> that it was the intention of Bonaparte to escape from Rochefort in a Danish sloop, concealed in a cask stowed in the ballast, with tubes so constructed as to convey air for his breathing. I afterwards inquired of General Savary, if there had been any foundation for such a report; when he informed me that the plan had been thought of, and the vessel in some measure prepared; but it was considered too hazardous; for had we detained the vessel for a day or two, he would have been obliged to make his situation known, and thereby forfeited all claims to the good treatment he hoped to ensure by a voluntary surrender.

The game was up. With no way out but via the British, Napoleon put a bold face on it and wrote a letter to the Prince Regent, whose father, George III, was at that time mentally incapacitated .

Rochefort, July 13th, 1815.

Your Royal Highness,

A victim to the factions which distract my country, and to the enmity of the greatest powers of Europe, I have terminated my political career, and I come, like Themistocles, to throw myself upon the hospitality of the British people. I put myself under the protection of their laws; which I claim from your Royal Highness, as the most powerful, the most constant, and the most generous of my enemies.

Napoleon

He came aboard with thirty-three people in his party, military men, dignitaries, their wives and children, servants and his own personal chef, while seventeen others were accommodated aboard another ship. Maitland offered up the great stern cabin of the ship. 'I propose,' he said, 'dividing (it) in two, that the ladies may have the use of one part of it.' But he was told, 'The Emperor will be better pleased to have the whole of the after-cabin to himself, as he is fond of walking about, and will by that means be able to take more exercise.' After Napoleon's first meal on board 'a cup of strong coffee' was handed round; he then rose and went into the after-cabin, asking all the party to accompany him, the ladies among the rest. After that first meal courtesy of the *Bellerophon*'s sea cooks, all Napoleon's subsequent meals were prepared by his own chef and kitchen and meals served off silver plates.

News of what was afoot had been sped to London by fast frigate – and faster still, back via Admiralty telegraph to Portsmouth and Plymouth. Every old seaman living along the route would watch the telegraph shutters open and close and although they could not read the codes, they knew the numbers that identified each ship-of-the-line and would have known that the old 'Billy Ruffian' as they called her, was coming in and many may have guessed that something was up.

The next two days were calm and sunny. 'Bonaparte amused himself by playing at cards after breakfast: the game was vingt-un, in which all the party joined, except myself,' said Maitland, a Scottish aristocrat of some wealth who could have made an outstanding career as a diplomat, which was probably the reason he had been assigned that specific patrol duty. 'He proposed that I should play with them, but I told him I had no money, making it a rule to leave it all with my wife before I went to sea: on which he laughed, and good-humouredly offered to lend me some, and trust me until we arrived in England: I, however, declined his offer, having the numerous duties of the ship to attend to.'

On Sunday, 23 July, Bonaparte remained upon deck a great part of the morning. He cast many a melancholy look at the coast of France, but made few observations on it. Maitland reports:

> About eight in the evening, the high land of Dartmoor was discovered, when I went into the cabin and told him of it: I found him in a flannel dressing-gown, nearly undressed, and preparing to go to bed. He put on his greatcoat, came out upon deck, and remained some time looking at the land; asking its distance from Torbay, and the probable time of our arrival there.

Perhaps he was also thinking of the French and American prisoners of war who had died there.

News of their arrival had preceded them and when they dropped anchor off Brixham on Monday, 24 July, Maitland made sure that the scores of small boats that began to encircle *Bellerophon* were kept at a safe distance. But Bonaparte seemed to relish the attention and came out on deck, waving his hat to the crowds. It was at this time that the artist, Charles Eastlake, who was Plymouth born and bred, came racing down from London to Devonport with his sketch pad – possibly tipped off to events by his father, who was a well-connected Admiralty lawyer in London. Risking life and limb, he managed to get close enough in a small skiff to make some lightning sketches of the man, as well as details of the colour of his clothing: details later verified in this letter, dated a week after the *Bellerophon* had left Torbay for good, by a young naval officer who had taken his wife, Emma, out to the ship. (Eastlake's picture now hangs in the National Maritime Museum, Greenwich.)

> Our boat (which was a very handsome one and filled with Ladies and Officers) having attracted his attention, he came forward and looked at us occasionally with an opera glass, for the space of five minutes. He was dressed in a green coat with red collar and cuffs and gold epaulettes and he wore a Star. After staying good naturedly long

enough to satisfy the curiosity of the ladies, he sat down to a writing table and we saw no more of him.

In a postscript to this eyewitness account, he adds:

I have been twice at St Helena and have dined often in the house which will be Napoleon's residence. It is a delightful spot and with half the comfort that he will have I could make my mind up to live some years there very easily …

The next day Maitland was ordered to sail round to Plymouth, where a higher level of security could be maintained. As *Bellerophon* waited the tide, Napoleon – unaware of the imminent move – 'walked above an hour on deck, frequently stood at the gangway, or opposite to the quarter-deck ports, for the purpose of giving the people an opportunity of seeing him, and, whenever he observed any well-dressed women, pulled his hat off, and bowed to them'. By the following week the *Plymouth Dock Newspaper* was evidently hot under the collar on the subject:

On Sunday, we regret to say, a large proportion of spectators, not only took off their hats, but cheered him; apparently with a view of soothing his fallen fortunes, and treating him with respect and consideration. His linen sent ashore to be washed, has been held in much esteem, that many individuals have temporarily put on his shirts, waistcoats and neckcloths. Blind infatuation! Our correspondent, who was alongside the Bellerophon on Sunday last, says that the sympathy in his favour was astonishing, that he heard no cheering, but that the hats of the men, and the handkerchiefs of the ladies, were waving in every direction.

Maitland continues his diary account:

He then spoke of the character of the fishermen and boatmen on our coast, saying, 'They are generally smugglers as well as fishermen; at one time a great many of them were in my pay, for the purpose of obtaining intelligence, bringing money over to France, and assisting prisoners of war to escape. They even offered, for a large sum of money, to seize the person of Louis, and deliver him into my hands; but as they could not guarantee the preservation of his life, I would not give my consent to the measure.'

The ship anchored off Plymouth Sound, and the frigates Liffey and Eurotas were anchored nearby, to row guard. No one was to come near the ship, let alone board it. Maitland picks up one of the consequences of his orders:

In the afternoon Sir Richard and Lady Strachan, accompanied by Mrs. Maitland, came alongside the ship. Bonaparte was walking the deck, and, when I told him my wife was in the boat, he went to the gangway, pulled off his hat, and asked her if she would not come up and visit him. She shook her head; and I informed him, that my orders were so positive, I could not even allow her to come on board. He answered, 'That is very hard.' And addressing himself to her, 'Lord Keith is a little too severe; is he not, Madam?' He then said to me, 'I assure you her portrait is not flattering; she is handsomer than it is.'

On Sunday, 30 July, there were reckoned to be upwards of a thousand small boats crowded round the ship, in each of which, on an average, there were not fewer than eight people. The crush was so great that the guard boats became desperate to keep them off; one chose simply to ram some of the smaller boats with such force as nearly to upset them, 'alarming the ladies and children extremely'. A man, a stone mason from Plymouth, was drowned. It was at about this time that Maitland ordered the firing of one of the ship's great guns as a warning to everyone to 'stand off!' It was also a this time that Napoleon knew for certain that he was not to be allowed to set foot in England but would, instead, be exiled to the island of St Helena:

The idea of it is perfect horror to me. To be placed for life on an island within the Tropics, at an immense distance from any land, cut off from all communication with the world, and every thing that I hold dear in it! It is worse than Tamerlane's iron cage. I would prefer being delivered up to the Bourbons. Among other insults but that is a mere bagatelle, a very secondary consideration – they style me General! They can have no right to call me General; they may as well call me Archbishop, for I was head of the church, as well as the army. If they do not acknowledge me as Emperor, they ought as First Consul; they have sent Ambassadors to me as such; and your King, in his letters, styled me brother.

As Bonaparte always retired early to bed, it was the custom for the French ladies and officers to assemble every evening in the ward room, and partake of wine and water, punch or bishop – a mixture consisting of port, Madeira, nutmeg and other ingredients, well known to sailors, and much relished by the French It was during one of these occasions that Napoleon's senior aide, General Bertrand, and his wife, the countess, entered into a great argument, which became so heated that they took it out onto the deck. She told him that she would sooner die than accompany him to St Helena and when he told her it was his duty she stormed below, pushed her way past the two Royal Marine sentries and threw herself at the feet of Napoleon. He is said to have looked amazed and told her that her husband was a free man – at which she ran to her own cabin and locked the door. Fortunately a French officer, seeing her distress, followed her, broke open the latch and found her halfway through the window in an attempt, not to escape, but to drown herself.

More drama followed. Information arrived from London that a *habeas corpus* writ had been taken out to summon Bonaparte as a witness to a hearing of some kind in London: a device simply to get him on shore. A lawyer was already on his way down to serve it and Maitland was therefore ordered to be ready to put to sea at a moment's notice.

Bonaparte was quick to note the activity and was told that they were to rendezvous with the *Northumberland*, the vessel appointed to take him to his final captivity. He said: 'I wanted nothing of them [the government] but hospitality, or, as the ancients would express it, "air and water". My only wish was to purchase a small property in England, and end my life there in peace and tranquility.'

Soon after nine o'clock, the *Bellerophon*'s signal was made and they beat out into the Sound with the guard boats towing them out against wind and tide. Thus Napoleon departed Devon, in enforced haste and in deep despair, never to return. He lived on St Helena for five and a half years until his death, from stomach cancer, at sunset on 5 May 1821. He told his faithful General Bertrand, who had accompanied him into exile, that, lifelong atheist that he was, he was not afraid to die, 'The only thing I am afraid of,' he added with a smile, 'is that the English will keep my body and put it in Westminster Abbey!' His body was exhumed on the orders of King Louis Phillipe I of France in 1840 and taken to Paris amidst great ceremony and his body now lies entombed within six coffins beneath a great slab of carved red porphyry, in the central crypt of the *Eglise du Dome* Church at the *Hotel des Invalides* in the heart of Paris. The tomb has a solemn, almost sacred, atmosphere and why not, commented William Makepeace Thackeray, 'for who is god here but Napoleon?'

In vain did two noble and extraordinary women, both bitterly betrayed by their husbands, come to live quietly in Devon at the beginning of the nineteenth century.

THE LADIES WHO LIVED ON THE HILL

As chance would have it, Frances Lady Nelson, wife of the naval hero, and Anne Lady Byron, wife of the poet, both came to live a few doors from each other at numbers 6 and 19 the Beacon, a genteel and secluded row of fine, newly built properties perched high above the then seaside fishing village of Exmouth.

But history had not finished with either of them, even after the deaths of their spouses: Nelson from his wounds at Trafalgar in 1805 and Byron, the poet, in 1824 from a fever during the Greek war of independence. Lady Nelson suffered tragedy upon tragedy, losing two husbands: her first, Dr Josiah Nisbet, to a fever contracted in the West Indies where she had first met and married him, the second to her 'Hero of the Nile' husband lost to the embrace of 'that woman', the notorious Emma Hamilton. But these events were only the beginning of suffering for a woman who never spoke ill of her husband and defended both his name and reputation throughout her life. Following her move to Exmouth, Frances lost not only her son by her first marriage – Josiah – but no fewer than four of her grandchildren, all of whom are buried with her at nearby Littleham, of which more anon.

Lady Byron's tragic lot was to lead to her fleeing with her infant daughter, Ada, when she believed, barely a year after her marriage, that she was wedded to a madman – a man whose countless well-documented sexual encounters with both men and women (including his half-sister Augusta, who bore him a son) would earn him the title of one who was 'mad, bad and dangerous to know'. Like her titled neighbour a few steps along the elegant terrace at the Beacon, Lady Anne never maligned her husband: unlike Byron, who slandered and wrote against her for the rest of his life, while she remained stoically silent – something that infuriated him. In fact, it was not until after her death that her friend and confidante, Harriet Beecher Stowe, the American author of *Uncle Tom's Cabin* and a lifelong campaigner against slavery and for the rights of married women, turned the tables on the Byron camp and spoke at length on behalf of her wickedly maligned friend in her book, *Lady Byron Vindicated*:

> During all this trial, strange to say, her belief that the good in Lord Byron would finally conquer was unshaken. To a friend who said to her, 'O, how could you love him!' she answered, briefly, 'My dear, there was the angel in him'. She read every work that Byron wrote, read it with a deeper knowledge than any human being but herself could possess. The ribaldry and the obscenity and the insults, with which he strove to make her ridiculous in the world, fell at her pitying feet unheeded.

So did those two ladies-in-exile on the sunny southern slopes of what was fast becoming one of Devon's favourite resorts, confide in each other, over the garden wall? Did Fanny and Annabella (Lady Byron's familiar name to her friends) share their innermost thoughts about their errant husbands? The answer is almost certainly 'no'. Although society was fuelled by gossip – then as now – Fanny and Annabella were both, first and foremost, ladies, and this a time of manners, decorum and the strict observance of the social graces that prohibited all such interchanges between people of breeding and rank, face to face across the tea cups. Instead they talked about the weather, their health, their children and, in Fanny's case, her grandchildren. Both performed good works, read books and newspapers, wrote letters (Annabella was a good poet in her own right), entertained in their homes (as well as local hotels) over teas and suppers and enjoyed the occasional promenade. They were regular visitors to the town and especially to Exmouth's new and popular Assembly Rooms at the bottom of the Beacon, which had become a magnet for local society. Both, of course, were also regular churchgoers and members of the congregation at the church of St Margaret and St Andrew at nearby Littleham.

Exmouth then had a population of 2,000 or so and was just fifteen hours' coach travel from Bath and twenty or less from London, and was cleaner and the bathing machines not easily overlooked by curious passers-by. The Nelsons had known both places well. They had spent part of their honeymoon to-ing and fro-ing between the newly emerging coastal resorts of east and south Devon. The year had been 1789, Fanny was then 28, and a widow with a young son, Josiah Nisbet. Her new husband, Nelson, was 31, and it was almost certainly this memory of happier times that brought her back, aged 46, after his passing.

Annabella arrived later in Exmouth and chose to live at No. 16, a property that was then a small but very select hotel. Her daughter Ada was brought up to study the sciences and logic – an unusual education for a woman in that era – in the hope that any artistic or poetic leanings or 'amorous excesses' inherited from her father in self-imposed exile, would not be allowed to flourish. Byron had died in 1824 when Ada was 8 years old and so determined was her mother to paint the father out of her daughter's life that she was not shown the family portrait of the man – which was kept hanging prominently wherever they lived, but covered in a green shroud – until her twentieth birthday.

Alas for Annabella's best efforts, his genius did manifest itself in his daughter, not as a writer of poetry but as a scientist or 'natural philosopher', to use the language of the age. She worked with Charles Babbage, the mathematician and inventor who lived in Totnes and designed and built the world's first 'calculating engine' or computer. He was also a philosopher and believed, interestingly enough, that many of the 'breakthroughs' in understanding by the scientific mind came about through divine revelation. Ada, mathematical genius that she was, agreed with him. She once wrote to a fellow scientist, 'I am often reminded of certain sprites and fairies one reads of, who are at one's elbows in one shape now, and the next minute in a form most dissimilar.' In spite of her mother's safeguarding, Ada was undoubtedly a chip off the old block.

But the Byrons were yet to arrive in Exmouth when, in 1815, the Napoleonic wars finally over, Fanny's son, Josiah (after a career in the Navy, where he had been the despair of his stepfather) was given £1,000 by his mother to set up a business. By 1819 he had extended its scope to Paris and on a return visit to Exmouth, met and married a personable young woman called Frances Evans, who had become companion to Lady Nelson at No. 6.

In 1823 Fanny went to Paris and stayed with Josiah and Frances and their young family in their home in the *Champs-Élysées* and did what most grandmothers are expected to do – baby sat while the parents travelled around Europe. But they were all together on Lake Geneva, where Fanny actually met Lord Byron, who took them rowing on the lake. To her horror, one of the little ones fell in and was saved from drowning by Byron, a strong swimmer, who dived in after the child.

Back in Exmouth, what is nowadays called Nelson House must have seemed suddenly large and empty to her, so she moved to a smaller property at the other end of the Beacon, in Louisa Terrace. Came 1830, and Fanny, now in her sixty-ninth year, was brought tragic news from France. Josiah, her only surviving child, had died suddenly, probably of heart failure brought on by 'dropsy' (oedema). She arranged for his body, together with three of his young children who had died previously and had been buried in a cemetery in Paris, to be exhumed and returned to Exmouth. As the coffins waited in the courtyard of a French convent there were riots, and Frances Nisbet and her remaining family were forced to flee the city, dressed as peasants. They managed to get back to England safely and made their way to Fanny's London home at No. 23 Harley Street.

Meanwhile, the four coffins came back to Exmouth unexpectedly and were landed at the Temple Steps. What to do? In his book *Exmouth Milestones*, Eric Delderfield writes:

The Customs House officer had them removed to the house of Mr. Edmund Weller, then being built but not completed on the sea front where Alston Terrace now joins it. Being circular in shape it was to be called Beach Castle but forever afterwards it became known locally as Corpse Castle and subsequently, when it was only frequented by the town's strays, as Cat's Castle and was always thought of as being haunted.

A year later, Fanny Nelson died at Harley Street on 4 May 1831, and who would say that it was not of a broken heart? Her body was brought from London and was buried beside her son and her grandchildren in the churchyard at Littleham. Her eldest grandchild, also called Fanny, later wrote of her grandmother's good nature and her devotion to her husband's memory, and said she often kissed a miniature of him. Lady Nelson once confided to her, 'When you are older little Fan, you may know what it is to have a broken heart.'

Lady Byron left Exmouth and returned to London. She too was to suffer the intense pain of outliving her only child. Ada died in 1852 after a long illness. She was 36 years old, the same age as her father, and at her written request is entombed in the Byron family vault at the church of St Mary Magdalene in Hucknall, Warwickshire. A portrait artist later wrote of the grieving mother, 'There is a lambent sorrow about her, bland and touching, but she was no more fit for him than a dove for a volcano, poor Lady Byron. She looks as though she saw an inward sorrow. Perhaps his sublime head is always haunting her imagination.' Byron's spirit it seems had haunted them both, wife and daughter, throughout their lives.

Our extraordinary weather in recent years has been nothing compared to the extraordinary goings-on of 1816.

THE LION ATTACK ON THE EXETER COACH

They called it 'the year without a summer' and it was also the origin of the expression 'eighteen hundred and frozen-to-death', and with good cause. That darkest of years was 1816, made even more memorable perhaps in the West of England that autumn when the Exeter mail coach was attacked by a starving lion.

It began in the year before, some 8,000 miles from Devon when Mount Tambora, a 13,000ft Indonesian volcano erupted on 10 April 1815. It killed tens of thousands of people in the immediate vicinity and unleashed climatic changes around the world that brought about the deaths of many thousands more. To this day, it stands as the world's worst recorded volcanic disaster, with 93 cubic miles of ash being spewed into the upper atmosphere within a few minutes, reducing the height of the mountain by 4,000ft. The ash clouds circled the globe in the upper atmosphere for two years, bringing unseasonal snows, floods and droughts to the northern hemisphere, followed by famines, pestilence and disease. All of these touched the

West Country, while some of the extraordinary sunsets triggered by the dust have been recorded in Turner's most memorable paintings. It rained in the West of England throughout that summer on 142 recorded days out of 153. There was snow on Dartmoor in June and lakes and ponds froze on high ground. Autumn came in cold, bleak and cheerless.

This then was the background to that one particular night in that extraordinary year, a cloudy but bitterly cold evening when the Exeter mail coach was attacked by a lion, or to be more precise, a lioness. This was the crack Quicksilver coach, which had left Devonport before the sun rose that chill Sunday morning of 20 October 1816, bound for London at a steady 10 to 12mph, via south Devon, Exeter, Salisbury and Andover, picking up and dropping off mails along the way.

Apart from the mails themselves – slim leather satchels kept securely in the boot – the coach was lightly loaded. People had come and gone as it rumbled across Devon, and by the time it reached Exeter there were just two people on board, both of them men and both seated inside. The only two souls braving the elements that short autumn day and long, bitterly cold night, were the coachman and the guard. The guard's duty was to stay with the coach from start to finish of the journey: the coachman, on the other hand, travelled 50 miles in one direction and then changed places with the coach coming in the opposite direction by stepping across the gap between the two. Thus these men were experts on the roads they travelled and knew each twist and turn like the backs of their hands.

The coach's lamps were lit at Shaftesbury as the sun set: two double-wicked road lamps to the front, showing that they were an approaching mail, two double-wicked lanterns on either side that dimly illuminated the ground for a yard or so to left and right of the passenger doors, and a small covered light positioned just in front of the guard. On that particular night this was one Joseph Pike, who sat at the very back of the coach facing a wide wooden box with a hinged lid.

As the only Post Office employee aboard the mail coach, Pike wore an official uniform of a black hat with a gold band and a scarlet coat with blue lapels and gold braid. All this beneath a greatcoat and scarf of his own purchase. His guard's light served three purposes. Firstly it enabled him to read 'London time' from the sealed chronometer, charged to his keeping by the Post Office and kept in a pouch slung around his neck; secondly it allowed him to sort the mail bags for each drop by reading their engraved brass labels, and thirdly, it kept his hands warm. At the bottom of the box were two pistols and a blunderbuss. Although 1785 was the last time a mail coach had been held up by a highwayman, an Act of Parliament decreed that they be kept fully loaded at all times.

The coachman, meanwhile, whose name has been lost in the mists of time, steered his team of four horses through the inky blackness of the night, his way lit periodically through cloud by the occasional glimpse of a star and a two-day-old new moon. But what we do know of him was common to all coachmen of that period. Seated on a sprung board at the front right of the coach where he took the brunt of the weather, he probably took a tipple or two along the road at each stop to keep out the cold. Tradition has it that he should wear a soft, wide-brimmed hat, sometimes held on by a long scarf that also wrapped twice round his neck before disappearing beneath a full-length overcoat. He wore calf-length leather boots and kept a short, sharp knife in the top of the right-hand boot, which was used for cutting traces should a horse fall or become entangled in its harness. He held the reins for all four horses in his left hand and as a consequence 'had a left-biceps like a cannon ball'. His right hand held the whip.

The Quicksilver's change of horses before their encounter with the lioness had been, ominously enough, at the still-renowned Red Lion Inn at Salisbury, where our nameless driver had come in earlier, driving the Devonport-bound coach. One Thomas Trollope (brother of Anthony Trollope) wrote of one of these rapid changeovers of mail coaches:

> It was a pretty sight to see the changing of the horses. There stood the fresh team, two on the off side, two on the near side, and the coach was drawn up with the utmost exactitude between them. Four ostlers jump to the splinter-bars and loose the traces; the reins have already been thrown down. The driver retains his seat, and, within the minute (more than once, within fifty seconds by the watch) the coach is again on its onward journey.

The lead horse on this occasion we know was called Pomegranate, formerly a race horse that had, according to Exeter's *Flying Post* (which reported the story just three days later), developed such a bad temper in the racing stables that he had been sold to the owner of the Red Lion, a Mr Weekes. After the change of horses, the Quicksilver soon left the flickering yellow lights of the ancient city behind and headed out into the night again and across Salisbury Plain in the direction of Andover. The next scheduled stop was the Winterslow Hut (later to become the Pheasant Inn), a lonely halt then, as now, and 'in the middle of nowhere', as that renowned man of letters, William Hazlitt later called it in the diary he kept when he lodged there.

As they crested the hill 7 miles or so further along what is nowadays the old A30 and began the long final descent towards the inn, Joseph Pike reached for his post horn, his 'three feet of tin', and gave it the regulatory three double blasts to warn them of their approach. The coachman could already see the yard at the front of the inn lit by lanterns and the small team of waiting ostlers who would change the team and get them on their way again. It was at this moment that Pike, looking down to his right, spied what he took to be 'a large calf' running alongside the coach and shouted a warning to the coachman. He in turn delivered a warning crack of his whip to whatever it was that was causing such distress to his 'cattle'.

It was now, as the Quicksilver pulled into the yard, that all hell broke loose. The lioness bounded forward and leaped on to the back of the offside leader, throwing its front paws round the neck of the terrified beast as it sank in tooth and claw. The horse, in its agony, reared and half fell to the right, almost toppling the coach, its front hooves lashing out in an attempt to free itself from the harness and deal with its attacker in the only way it could. Amid the terrified screams of the rearing horses and the shouts of the people in the yard, both coachman and guard now saw the attacker as a lion. As the ostlers ran for their lives, the two coach passengers leapt from its nearside door, fled into the inn, ran up the staircase immediately in front of them and locked and barricaded the door of the first room they could find. The brave coachman shouted to Pike for the gun and began to clamber down from the wildly rocking coach, reaching for his short-bladed knife. Pike made a grab for the loaded blunderbuss in the box at his feet, and leaped from his seat. As his feet touched the ground and he straightened he turned to see a wild-faced man pointing a loaded pistol at his forehead.

'For God's sake don't kill her!' the man shouted. It was his lioness, the man screamed. She had escaped from his travelling menagerie and had cost him £500 and was 'as tame as a rabbit' if he and his men could only get to her. At this point, two men who had come running up with the owner released a mastiff dog, which leapt on to the lioness and sank its teeth into one of its hind legs. The lioness now turned its attention to the dog and seems to have quickly dispatched the poor creature, killing it outright and dragging it off into the darkness towards a wooden barn or granary towards the rear of the inn.

What then followed was subsequently reported in the *Salisbury and Winchester Journal*:

> Her owner and his assistants, after a short deliberation, followed her upon their hands and knees, with lighted candles, and having placed a sack on the ground near her, they made her lie down upon it; they then tied her four legs and passed a cord round her mouth, which they secured; in this state they drew her out from under the granary, upon the sack, and then she was lifted and carried by six men into her den in the caravan. To the astonishment of everyone who beheld this part of the transaction (which lasted about a quarter of an hour), the lioness lay as quietly as a lamb during her removal to the caravan; but when she was there she became sensible of the restraints she was under, and her rage was excessive till the cords which annoyed her were loosened.

Did those two extraordinary coachmen take a tot of brandy to settle their nerves after such an encounter? You can bet they did, but it is testimony to the importance they attached to their duty and the efficiency of the postal service at the time that the whole incident only delayed the mail coach by forty-five minutes before it changed teams completely, reinstated the two fleeing passengers from their locked upper room and continued on their route to London.

Pomegranate recovered and was bought from Mr Weekes by the enterprising menagerie owner, George Ballard, who exhibited the pair of animals at Salisbury Fair that same week and many other fairs over the following years. Ballard's Grand Collection of Wild Beasts was still doing the rounds. In 1826, ten years after the lion attack, the Quicksilver was still making the same run which, leaving Piccadilly at 8 p.m., arrived at Exeter at 12.34 the next day. Journey time? Sixteen hours, thirty-four minutes. Going on to Devonport, it arrived at 5.14 p.m., or twenty-one hours, fourteen minutes from London. There were no fewer than twenty-three changes of horse over the 216 miles and four changes of coachman. The cost of the cheapest single fare for an 'inside' passenger was 4 old pennies per mile, plus 20 old shillings in tips to the coachmen and guard (virtually obligatory), plus the cost of food and drink on the brief stopovers.

Pictured at Scrooge's shoulder is Charles Dickens himself, speaking through Fred, the character he created to put us right about Christmas.

DICKENS' CHRISTMAS PRESENT TO THE WEST OF ENGLAND

Charles Dickens did not invent 'traditional', old-fashioned Christmases of course, the kind that many of us still enjoy revelling in today (and so beloved of greetings card manufacturers): that particular garland rests more fittingly on the noble brow of Victoria's husband, Prince Albert. His wholesale import of the age-old German Christmas, complete with feasting, merriment and the lighted tree itself, hung with sugar plums and barley sugar canes, was readily embraced by the new, romantic era, ushered in by its new queen with her young family.

But it was Dickens, that literary genius and social commentator of the Victorian age, who not only promoted Christmas in this form, he did so by creating his immortal morality tale, *A Christmas Carol*. Having lived and worked in Devon as a young newspaper reporter, he returned to the county at the height of his fame to give one of the first ever public readings of this perennial classic in August 1858 at the Royal Public Rooms, in the heart of the city of Exeter. He afterwards wrote to his sister-in-law that the good people of Devon packed the place to the rafters and he wished that he had been able to book the venue again:

> We had a most wonderful night at Exeter. I think they were the finest audience I have ever read to. I don't think I have ever read, in some respects, so well, and I never beheld anything like the personal affection which they poured out upon me at the end. It was really a remarkable sight, and I shall always look back upon it with pleasure.

The reporter from the *Flying Post* was impressed by the great man's performance, as well he might:

> Mr. Dickens possesses great dramatic ability, wonderful powers of facial expression, and a rich sonorous voice, of which he is a perfect master – changing it from the rough tones of Scrooge to the sweet and delicate key of Tiny Tim with an easy and remarkable facility.

Yet, more than a century and a half after that Devon reading of *A Christmas Carol*, when that crowd streamed out into the High Street, laughing and crying in turn at the end of the performance, it still seems an extraordinary way for such a story to begin – as well as a unique use of a colon so early on in the first line of any piece of English literature.

> Marley was dead: to begin with. There is no doubt whatever about that. The register of his burial was signed by the clergyman, the clerk, the undertaker, and the chief mourner. Scrooge signed it. And Scrooge's name was good upon 'Change, for anything he chose to put his hand to. Old Marley was as dead as a door-nail.

Extraordinary, that is, until we are reminded of the novel's subtitle, often dropped by publishers in later editions: 'A Christmas Carol. In Prose. Being a Ghost Story of Christmas'.

Devon's winter weather in the early and mid-1800s, like most of the rest of southern England, was extreme. Sheep on Dartmoor were still being dug out of snowdrifts as late as April on successive years in the 1830s. Stagecoaches and their unfortunate passengers had to be rescued from monumental snowdrifts, roads were made impassable and rural communities were sometimes cut off for weeks at a time. In 1814, when Dickens was just 2 years old, the Thames had frozen over in London and its citizens marked the event with the Great Frost Fair, which saw coaches travelling on the frozen river between the City and Westminster while an elephant promoted a circus by being walked to and fro across the ice at Blackfriars. It has been suggested that these and similar weather-related events during his formative childhood years – before his father was torn away from the family and thrown into debtors' prison – made a deep and lasting impression on him that manifested in many of his writings, particularly in *The Pickwick Papers* and most pointedly in *A Christmas Carol* itself. Was the book then really an invocation of his childhood of Christmases with his family? Many believe that it is.

Dickens quit his life as a reporter in 1834, bid farewell to his drinking companions at the Turk's Head tavern next to Exeter's Guildhall and left Devon for London, to write full time. But he came back to the county often and married Catherine Hogarth, a pretty Scottish lass then living in Exeter and the daughter of his one-time newspaper editor. Dickens was 24 and she just 21.

It was 1836, the same year that he had published his first literary success, *The Pickwick Papers*. (The character of The Fat Boy is based on a potman at the Turk's Head.) Within a few years he had become an international literary celebrity, but although the couple had ten children the marriage was not a happy one. Nevertheless, Catherine found time, between her confinements, to write her own bestseller – a cookery book – which in an age of long book titles was called *What Shall we Have for Dinner? Satisfactorily Answered by Numerous Bills of Fare for from Two to Eighteen Persons.*

Catherine Dickens died on 22 November 1879 aged 64 and was laid to rest in Highgate Cemetery in London with her infant daughter, Dora, who had died in 1851 aged nearly 8 months. Charles John Huffam Dickens preceded her on 9 June 1870, aged 58. His grave is to be found at Poets' Corner, Westminster Abbey, but his greatest monument, of course, is his literary work. Of these, *A Christmas Carol* remains the most popular, internationally. As a book it has never been out of print.

On television it has appeared scores of times and in various guises since it was first transmitted by a New York television channel, WABD, on 20 December 1944. There have been twenty-two film versions since the first one-reeler attempted to tell the tale in 1901. That is, if you include *The Muppet Christmas Carol* (1992) with Michael Caine as Scrooge and Kermit the Frog as Bob Cratchit. But to the arguably sublime from the wonderfully ridiculous, the last words on this subject must surely go to the great man himself.

'If I could work my will,' said Scrooge indignantly, 'every idiot who goes about with "Merry Christmas" on his lips, should be boiled with his own pudding, and buried with a stake of holly through his heart. He should!'

But here, finally, is Charles Dickens himself, speaking to the reader in the voice of one of the key characters of the tale. Fred. Fred? You will remember (or might care to know) that Ebenezer Scrooge had a sister, called Fran, who had died in childbirth, bringing this, her only child, into the world. Having tried, unsuccessfully, to persuade his uncle to join him and his wife to share Christmas dinner with them, Fred tells the unrepentant old miser:

> The only time I know of, in the long calendar of the year, when men and women seem by one consent to open their shut-up hearts freely, and to think of people below them as if they really were fellow-passengers to the grave, and not another race of creatures bound on other journeys. And therefore, uncle, though it has never put a scrap of gold or silver in my pocket, I believe that it has done me good, and will do me good; and I say, God bless it!

Thirty years after slavery was abolished in the British Empire the first shipload of kidnapped South Sea Islanders was herded on to an Australian dockside by 'blackbirders' to open a sad new era of forced labour that is largely glossed over in our history books.

THE BISHOP AND THE SLAVERS

There is no known grave for Bishop John Coleridge Patteson. He was clubbed to death by natives on the island of Nukapu in the Solomon Islands on 20 September 1871 and after his palm-wrapped body was found later, floating in a canoe, he was buried at sea. He had left his home in Feniton, Devon, as a young priest and spent the rest of his life as a missionary, fighting the slave trade in the South Seas, which was plagued by ruthless gangs, who practised so-called 'blackbirding', kidnapping natives and selling them in Queensland, Australia, and Fiji to work on sugar and pineapple plantations.

Patteson has two monuments. One is made of brick and stone and stands at the crossroads between Feniton and Ottery St Mary on the old Honiton to Exeter road. The other is that his name and memory are celebrated in Anglican churches for his saintly life and as a martyr; he is commemorated with a Lesser Festival on 20 September.

John Coleridge Patteson was born in 1827 and grew up in Feniton. He was the elder son of Sir John Patteson and Frances Duke Coleridge, a niece of the poet, and was known to family and friends alike as 'Coley'. After three years at the King's School, Ottery St Mary, he was sent first to Eton and then to Balliol College, Oxford. A gifted linguist (he would eventually become fluent in twenty-three native tongues in Melanesia), he toured Europe before returning to Oxford in 1852, where he became a fellow of Merton College. He returned to his beloved Devon in September 1853, where he was ordained as a deacon and curate of the little church of St James and St Anne at Alfington and a year later was ordained a priest at Exeter Cathedral by the Rt Hon Rev Henry Phillpotts, Bishop of Exeter and a man who, until the Abolition of Slavery Act in 1833, had profited from the employment of 655 slaves in Jamaica. But that, as they say, is another story.

Patteson was 27 and was already looking beyond Devon to what would become his life's work. By the following March the young priest found himself on board a ship bound for Auckland, New Zealand, and would never see England again. He had been recruited to become a missionary in the South Seas by George Selwyn, himself the first Bishop of New Zealand, and for five years Patteson toured the islands on the good ship *Southern Cross*, learning the many languages spoken by the islanders, running the Melanesian Mission in Auckland and founding a college for boys on Norfolk Island. These were dark days in the islands, which were plagued by 'blackbirders' who kidnapped men, women and children and sold them into slavery (a healthy male could fetch £4 in 1863), especially to Fiji and Queensland where there were vast pineapple plantations. He was consecrated as the first Bishop of Melanesia in 1861 but with a diocese nearly 1,800 miles across he spent much of his day-to-day work making first contact with islanders by determining to look as little like an Anglican bishop as he could. When he reached a new island he would go barefoot, stripping down to shirt and trousers, rolled up to the knee. Then he would lower himself gently over the side of the ship's boat, which then waited offshore while he swam to the beach wearing his bishop's top hat: a top hat filled with small presents for the people.

He had what was described by his cousin and biographer, the novelist Charlotte Mary Yonge, as a grave and gentle face, a ready smile and a good memory for names and faces, which he could employ on subsequent visits. He wrote grammars and vocabularies and translated the gospels into the Mota language. Usually Patteson's gentle, quiet manner reassured the indigenous peoples, but not always. Once when he and his assistants were about to leave Santa Cruz, they were attacked. Despite Patteson's care for them, both of his companions died from the wounds they received from poisoned arrows. In 1867 the Melanesian Mission moved to Norfolk Island, where in the milder climate the school could not only continue in the winter months but native foods such as yams could be grown. Dynamic and practical, he taught the Mission to speak English, play cricket and tend livestock. But the visits to the island were becoming yearly more dangerous. In 1869 he wrote:

Vessels which have been taking away S. Sea islanders for the Fiji & Queensland labour market have acted in a very sad miserable way … often with treachery and violence. The effect is … to embitter the islanders against any white man whom they do not as yet know well to be their friend.

When his own end came, it was out of a clear blue sky, on the island of Nukapu. The log of the *Southern Cross* showed that they were in 9 fathoms of water beyond the reef, it was 91 degrees and 11.30 on the morning of 20 September 1871, the equatorial midsummer eve. This is how his scholar, Edward Wogale, reported events:

The ship's boat took him to some waiting canoes. There was a delay of about twenty minutes; and then two canoes went with the one containing the Bishop, the two chiefs, Moto and Taula, who had before been so friendly to him, being in them. The tide was so low that it was necessary to wade over the reef, and drag the canoes across to the deeper lagoon within. The boat's crew could not follow; but they could see the Bishop land on the beach, and there lost sight of him.

The boat had been about half-an-hour drifting about in company with the canoes, and there had been some attempt at talk, when suddenly, at about ten yards off, without any warning, a man stood up in one of them, and calling out, 'Have you anything like this?' Shot off one of the yard-long arrows, and his companions in the other two canoes began shooting as quickly as possible, calling out, as they aimed, 'This for New Zealand man! This for Bauro man! This for Mota man!' The boat was pulled back rapidly and was soon out of range but not before three out of the four had been struck; James only escaped by throwing himself back on the seat, while an arrow had nailed John's cap to his head, Mr. Atkin had one in his left shoulder, and poor Stephen lay in the bottom of the boat, with six arrows in the chest and shoulders.

(The rescue party from the ship) had long to wait till the tide was high enough to carry them across the reef, and they could see people on shore, at whom they gazed anxiously with a glass. About half-past four it became possible to cross the reef, and then two canoes rowed towards them: one cast off the other and went back; the other, with a heap in the middle, drifted towards them, and they rowed towards it.

As they came up with it, and lifted the bundle wrapped in matting into the boat. The boat came alongside, and two words passed, 'The body!' Then it was lifted up, and laid across the skylight, rolled in the native mat, which was secured at the head and feet. The placid smile was still on the face; there was a palm leaf fastened over the breast (in which were five knots tied – the number of the slain, as they supposed, or possibly of those whom his death was meant to avenge) and when the mat was opened there were five wounds, no more. [There then followed a description of the wounds which revealed that death was probably instantaneous.]

Charlotte Yonge surmised:

All this is an almost certain indication that his death was the vengeance for five of the natives. 'Blood for blood' is a sacred law, almost of nature, wherever Christianity has not prevailed, and a whole tribe is held responsible for the crime of one. Five men in Fiji are known to have been stolen from Nukapu; and probably their families believed them to have been killed, and believed themselves to be performing a sacred duty when they dipped their weapons in the blood of the Bishop whom they did not know well enough to understand that he was their protector.

The next morning, St Matthew's Day, the body of John Coleridge Patteson was committed to the waters of the Pacific. He was 44 years old. Yonge concludes:

There is pain too in telling the further fate of Nukapu. H.M.S. Rosario, (an 11-gun screw sloop sent to the Australia station to bring an end to 'blackbirding') Commander Markham, touched at Norfolk Island, and Captain Markham undertook at once to go to the island and make enquiries. A protest was drawn up and signed by all the members of the Mission against any attempt to punish the natives for the murder; and Captain Markham, a kind, humane, and conscientious man, as no one can doubt, promised that nothing of the kind should be attempted. But the natives could not but expect retaliation for what they had done. There was no interpreter. They knew nothing of flags of truce; and when they saw a boat approaching, full of white men, armed, what could they apprehend but vengeance for 'Bisope'?

So they discharged a volley of arrows, and a sergeant of marines was killed. This was an attack on the British flag, and it was severely chastised with British firearms. It is very much to be doubted whether Nukapu will ever understand that her natives were shot, not for killing the Bishop, but for firing on the British flag.

Stand on that table and smile for the gentlemen!

WIFE FOR SALE!

It was once thought legal by many country folk in rural Devon that a man could sell his wife at public auction, providing certain procedures were adhered to.

These included putting a straw halter round her neck and leading her – gently – to the auction, having first announced publicly that both parties were agreed to end the marriage in this way, and importantly that the wife would then be bound to transfer her affections to the highest bidder. Some wives went for a few pounds or even a few shillings: others for a pint of ale or a jug of gin or, in one case, a few shillings and a dog. The bid accepted, it was necessary for the buyer to then lead his new 'wife' home by that same bridle and not remove it until the couple had crossed the threshold of her new abode. This, they believed, made everything legal and above board.

This 'quaint' rural custom persisted in some parts of Devon, especially mid and north Devon (less so in the south) until shortly before the Great War, the last wife sale in the county being recorded in the early 1900s by the Rev. Sabine Baring-Gould, the vicar of St Peter's Church, Lewtrenchard, near Okehampton.

He was an extraordinarily gifted man, happily married with a large family, an author, a poet, a gatherer of folk songs and a composer who wrote 'Onward, Christian Soldiers'. His was an ancient Devon family and his lifelong study of the county, its people and customs was extensive and he recorded and wrote about what he saw and heard throughout his long life (1834–1924).

On the subject of wife sales he wrote that 'many such sales have taken place, and that this is so is due to rooted conviction in the rustic mind that such a transaction is legal and morally permissible'. When he was a boy, he recalled, there was a man in his parish called Henry Frise who was 'a village poet'. His verses, taken to the manor house, were rewarded with his dinner and a crown. He once used half of one of those payments to buy a wife at Okehampton market. Her name was Anne and, having bid half a crown for her, he led her still in her halter the 12 miles to his home, 'she placidly, contentedly wearing the loop about her neck'.

'I must say that Anne proved an excellent "wife". She was thrifty, clean, and managed a rough-tempered and rough-tongued man with great tact, and was generally respected. She died in or about 1843.'

Baring-Gould also recalled a publican who bought his wife for a stone 2 gallon jar of Plymouth gin. She had belonged to a stonecutter, who became dissatisfied with her and put up a written notice in several public places to this effect:

NOTICE

This here be to hinform the publick as how James Cole be dispozed to sell his wife by Auction. Her be a dacent, clanely woman, and be of age twenty-five ears. The sale be to take place in the New Inn, Thursday next at seven o'clock.

He held the sale, making the woman stand on a table, and he armed himself with a little hammer. The biddings were to be in kind and not in money. One man offered a coat, but as he was a small man and the seller was stout, when he found that the coat would not fit him, he refused it. Another offered a 'phisgie', i.e. a pick, but this also was declined, as the husband possessed a 'phisgie' of his own. Finally, the landlord offered a 2 gallon jar of gin, and down fell the hammer with 'Gone!'

Henry Whitfield, in his book *Plymouth and Devonport in Times of War and Peace* (1900), writes of how, in December 1822, the Plymouth town crier was sent out and about in Modbury market to announce that James Brooks was about to dispose of his wife by public auction. The lady was advertised as young and handsome and would arrive at the auction on horseback at precisely midday. Sure enough the lady arrived, attended by the ostler of the Lord Exmouth public house, and the husband invited the bidding. The first was for 5 shillings, then the sums offered mounted slowly to £2., whereupon the ostler called out, 'Three pounds!' and she would have been knocked down to him had not two town watchmen intervened and escorted the pair to the Guildhall, followed by a crowd.

When the mayor took them to task, the husband declared that for the life of him he could not see that he was doing wrong. He and his wife had agreed to the sale, as they had not lived together for long, and were ill-assorted, and therefore desired fresh partners. It transpired that the ostler was buying her at a reserved price, at which she had valued herself. There was a gentleman, the lady said, a Mr. K., whom she had expected to turn up and bid for her. 'I was very much annoyed,' she told the mayor, 'to find that he had not kept his promise. But I was so determined to be loosed from Mr. Brooks, that when Mr. K. did not attend, I asked the ostler to buy me with my own money.' The justices bound the loveless pair over in sureties to be of good behaviour, and dismissed them.

The Rev. W.H. Thornton, vicar of North Bovey, recalled:

In March of this year (1906), I was investigating in North Devon a remarkable instance of suicide, and a still more remarkable verdict thereon. My informant was an old poacher and fisherman, and speaking of the deceased, he said casually that he came of a curious family, and that he himself could well remember to have seen the dead man's grandfather leading his grandmother on a halter to be sold by public auction in Great Torrington Market. The reserve price was fixed at eighteen pence, but as no one would give so much money, the husband had to take his wife home again and resume matrimonial intercourse. Children were born to them, and the ultimate result was the suicide.

The reverend gentleman went on to say that shortly before he became the incumbent at North Bovey in 1868:

> a man, whose name I can give, walked into Chagford, and there by private agreement sold his wife to another man for a quart of beer. When he returned home with the purchaser the woman repudiated the transaction, and, taking her two children with her, went off at once to Exeter, and only came back to attend her husband's funeral, at which, unless I am mistaken, I officiated.

Devon was not the only scene of these wife sales, writes Baring-Gould, though they were probably more common here than elsewhere, and listed several other instances 'to relieve Devon of exclusive discredit in such matters'. In 1832 a farmer in Carlisle named Joseph Thomson sold his wife of three years for 20*s* and a Newfoundland dog. He placed her on a chair, with a rope of straw round her neck and then, according to the editor of the *Carlisle Annual Register*, made the following announcement:

> 'GENTLEMEN, I have to offer to your notice, my wife, Mary Anne Thomson, otherwise Williams, whom I mean to sell to the highest and fairest bidder. Gentlemen, it is her wish as well as mine to part for ever. She has been to me only a born serpent. I took her for my comfort, and the good of my home; but she became my tormentor, a domestic curse. Gentlemen, I speak the truth from my heart when I say may God deliver us from troublesome wives and frolicsome women! Avoid them as you would a mad dog, or a roaring lion, a loaded pistol, cholera morbus, Mount Etna, or any other pestilential thing in nature. Now I have shown you the dark side of my wife, and told you her faults and failings, I will introduce the bright and sunny side of her, and explain her qualifications and goodness. She can read novels and milk cows; she can laugh and weep with the same ease that you could take a glass of ale when thirsty. She can make butter and scold the maid; she can sing Moore's melodies, and plait her frills and caps; she cannot make rum, gin, or whisky, but she is a good judge of the quality from long experience in tasting them. I therefore offer her with all her perfections and imperfections for the sum of fifty shillings.

An hour later she was knocked down to one Henry Mears, for 20*s* and a Newfoundland dog. Mr and Mrs Thomson then parted company in perfect good humour, Mears and his new 'wife' one way, Thomson, his 20*s* and the dog the other.

Finally, and in complete contrast, there is the extraordinary instance of Mrs Anne Jeffries, a chambermaid at the Pelican Inn, Newbury, who was unhappily married to a Mr Jeffries, the ostler there. It was the late 1730s when Lord Henry Brydges, second Duke of Chandos, having stopped off at the inn to dine while on his way to London, had his meal interrupted by a commotion in the inn yard. Jeffries the ostler had led his wife into the yard with a halter round her neck and was offering her up for sale. So smitten with Anne's beauty 'and the patient way she waited to be set free from her ill-conditioned husband', and notwithstanding that he was already married, the good Duke bought her for himself for half a crown (12½p). She was his mistress for some years. In August 1738 his wife died, and by 1744 the ostler was dead also, and so the two were finally married in London on Christmas Day 1744. A noble contemporary said of her, 'Of her person and character people speak variously, but all agree that both were very bad.' She died in 1759, after which Chandos married again. Of the noble duke it was the king himself, George II, who said, 'There goes a hot headed, passionate, half-witted coxcomb.' So, hardly a love match there then.

But if you seek a happy ending in the midst of all these terrible goings-on, you should look no further than to the life and love of the Reverend Sabine Baring-Gould himself, who did so much to record them for posterity. When he was a very young curate he met Grace Taylor, the daughter of a mill hand, then aged 14. In the next few years they fell in love. His vicar, John Sharp, arranged for Grace to live for two years with relatives in York, 'to learn middle-class manners'. He and Grace were married in 1868, they had fifteen children and their marriage lasted until her death forty-eight years later. When he buried his wife in 1916 he had carved on her tombstone the Latin motto *Dimidium Animae Meae*, which translates as 'Half my Soul'. He did not remarry and died on 2 January 1924 at their home at Lewtrenchard. He is buried there at St Peter's Church, next to his wife.

A brief voyage around Dartmouth's Royal Naval College is a tour of a building designed as a ship.

RULE BRITANNIA!

At first glance it may not look much like a ship, perched high and dry on a hill overlooking Devon's beautiful Dart Estuary, but this is the Britannia Royal Naval College (BRNC): the initial officer training establishment of the Royal Navy – and before it was a building, it was a ship, one of the wooden walls of England.

This was in 1863 when the first 'college', the wooden hulk HMS *Britannia*, was towed from Portland and moored in the river. A year later, after an influx of new recruits, *Britannia* was supplemented by HMS *Hindustan*. Thus, Dartmouth can lay claim to its training role for more than 150 years.

Sir Aston Webb (1849–1930), who designed the shore-based college, was one of the greatest architects of his era. In addition to the BRNC, he also designed the Victoria & Albert Museum, Admiralty Arch and The Mall, opening up to present the imposing remodelled facade of Buckingham Palace itself. He was aware that the bricks-and-mortar college needed to maintain the excellence inherited from the spirit and traditions that had shaped the men of the nation's senior service in the cradle of the old warships that had preceded it. So he studied the plans of the old wooden-walls-turned-places-of-learning, their layouts, uses and functions as he created the new BRNC at Dartmouth. It provided classrooms, drill halls, workshops, mess decks, a quarterdeck and sleeping quarters for generations of naval officers.

His building – opened in 1905, 100 years after Trafalgar – is a remarkable structure and contains what is almost certainly the most extraordinary 'secret' design built into a piece of architecture anywhere in Britain – certainly since Stonehenge – and further afield, most probably since the Temple of Ramesses the Great at Abu Simbel.

Like the college, each of those places is aligned by their architects in such a way that at a given time of day and at specific time of year, heaven itself, in the form of the sun, is harnessed to bring illumination to a precise spot and for a particular reason. At Stonehenge it is the sunrise on midsummer morning kissing the altar stone. In Dartmouth it is Nelson, of immortal memory, whose untimely death at the Battle of Trafalgar is honoured in this way. And the man who made the calculations and designed the entire structure around that single event was the magician, Aston Webb.

Once a year, on Trafalgar Day, 21 October, in the half-light of the chapel a beam of sunlight travels down and onto the altar from a small round window high above the west door. This year's 21 October will be the same as last year. Those who have come to remember all the Royal Navy's fallen remain silent, facing the altar, their minds taken back particularly to the deck of *Victory*, when Nelson fell.

Nelson's flagship, *Victory*, is locked in a deadly struggle alongside the French battleship *Redoubtable*. It is almost 1.15 in the afternoon. Captain Hardy and Nelson, in full uniform, are walking on the upper deck through the midst of the intense fighting, both ships shaking with the intensity of broadside after broadside. Suddenly Hardy realises that Nelson is not by his side. He turns to see him kneeling on the deck, supporting himself with his hand, before falling onto his side. He has been shot by a marksman from the fighting top of the French ship and his spine is shattered. Nelson is carried below by sergeant major of Marines Robert Adair and two seamen. As he is lifted, he has them drape a handkerchief over his face so that any crew who see him will not be alarmed. He will die below decks some three hours later, and it is at this point – and at this time – that the sun touches the altar in commemoration, marked in the very fabric of the chapel each year.

Leave the chapel and here again is Webb's guiding hand, seen once more in the long corridor that serves as the backbone of the main building. He uses it to make distinct the two important aspects of a cadet's life in service. At one end is the chapel (the spiritual), at the other the so-called gunroom (the temporal). But if you are looking for guns in the gun room you will be disappointed. A gunroom is the junior officers' mess on a naval vessel and was originally the quarters of the gunner. The senior officers' equivalent is the wardroom, where traditionally naval etiquette demanded that the three subjects of politics, religion and ladies were taboo. Quite how this works in practice in wardrooms (or gunrooms) in today's Royal Navy is unclear, where more than 10 per cent of all officers nowadays are female (so too are all ratings). Officer training for the Women's Royal Naval Service – the WRNS – moved from Greenwich to Dartmouth in the 1970s and became fully integrated with the men in the early 1990s.

But there were many Wrens in service at Dartmouth during the Second World War, one of whom, Petty Officer Ellen Whittal, lost her life in an air raid – but not before she had been instrumental in saving the lives of hundreds of cadets and officers who had routinely arrived as the new intake in early September. Mrs Ellen Victoria Whittal, 'Nella' to her family, had been instructed to send letters and telegrams to each of these men ordering them to delay their arrival by a week. Why the change of plan? In the years following the war the official line was – and remains – that putting off the date of starting the term was simply a means of adjusting the end of term to coincide with Christmas leave. But inevitably, speculation and controversy remain. This start date for the arrival of the new intake was a tradition – only adjusted marginally by leap years and calendar adjustments. Had Ellen Whittal not carried out her orders to the letter, how many lives would have been lost when the great gathering place at the college, called the Quarterdeck, directly under a roof of several hundreds of tons of Cornish slate, came crashing down?

Six Focke-Wulf Fw 190s launched their attack at about 11.30 a.m. on Friday, 18 September 1942, out of the sun and at low level. They hit shipping in the river, the shipyard on the opposite bank and the college itself. Although twenty-five people died that day and more than forty were injured, Ellen Whittal was the only person to lose her life in the college itself. She was cremated at Plymouth City Crematorium, and her name appears on the memorial in Plymouth (Efford) Cemetery.

Staff and students were moved to Eaton Hall in Cheshire for the rest of the war, the damage was repaired and BRNC taken over by the US Navy as its HQ in the run-up to the invasion of Europe in 1944.

Three times they pulled the trapdoor, three times it failed to open.

THE MAN THEY COULDN'T HANG

John 'Babbacombe' Lee was probably not guilty of the murder of his employer, Emma Keyse, at her home in Babbacombe on 15 November 1884.

The evidence against him was weak and circumstantial, but with a previous criminal record for robbery and Lee – apparently – the only man in the house at the time of the horrendous killing, the jury at his trial at the Guildhall in Exeter found him guilty and he was sentenced to be 'hanged by the neck until dead'. Yet he continued to profess his innocence all the way to the gallows. But as events unfolded on that grey morning of 23 February 1885, with hundreds of people standing in the cold outside Exeter Prison waiting for the official notice of his execution to be pinned to the door, Lee was about to escape death at the hangman's noose and take his place in British criminal history as 'the man they couldn't hang'. For in spite of three attempts by the vastly experienced public executioner, James Berry, the trapdoor beneath Lee's feet failed to open, not once, not twice but three times. Lee walked back to his cell, where he told the priest that he had dreamt all of this the night before and knew that he would be spared death. Victorian society was rocked by the news and 'his escape from the very jaws of death' was held up as proof, provided by Providence, of his innocence. Subsequently Lee's sentence would be reduced to life imprisonment – and eventually, after twenty-two years of appeals – freedom.

John Henry George Lee was born in Abbotskerswell in 1864, and put out to work by his father when he was 15. He found a job as a servant at the Glen, the large house of a Miss Emma Keyse in Babbacombe, before he left suddenly to join the Navy at Plymouth – to his father's anger, his mother's distress and Miss Keyse's sad regret. Invalided out with pneumonia at 18, he became a footman in Babbacombe but shortly after was arrested and jailed for robbing an employer. On release however, he was reinstated by Miss Keyse as a general handyman. Two elderly servants also lived at the Glen, sisters Eliza and Jane Neck, and Elizabeth Harris, the cook and Lee's stepsister. He slept in the pantry, the rest of the household upstairs.

During the night of Saturday, 15 November 1884, someone started a fire at the house and panic ensued. Miss Keyse was not in her bedroom and was found by Lee in the smoke-filled dining room – but only after he had smashed a window with his elbow to clear the smoke, cutting his arm in the process. In evidence he later said what he saw as he turned: 'My poor dear mistress lying on the carpet – a ghastly sight. I can still see her eyes staring out from the hair which had fallen about her face. I can still see her hands. They were blue and claw-like, drawn up in convulsions of death.'

Miss Keyse's throat had been cut and her head savagely mutilated with an axe or some such instrument. Oil had been poured over her body and an attempt made to burn it. Lee helped the police carry the body from the house, before he was apprehended on suspicion of murder. They had found a knife in Lee's sleeping area that he could not explain. This, together with the cut on Lee's arm and blood on a trouser leg – this in an age when forensic science had still to be developed – were sufficient for Lee to be arrested and sent for trial.

James Berry, the hangman, was born in 1852, in Yorkshire. He was married and had six children, three of whom died when they were young. He became a policeman for eight years in his early 20s but after eight years he left the force and, having met the public executioner during his police days, he was persuaded to apply for and got the job of public executioner, chosen from some 1,400 applicants. He was 32 years old and over the next eight years he hanged 131 people, including five women. He was paid £10 per hanging plus expenses, second-class rail and cab fares and hotel. He was by all accounts a quiet and contemplative man, his favourite occupations being fishing and otter hunting. Frequently when going to an execution in a country town he took his rod and basket, and took half a day to fish before or after the execution. At home, he kept rabbits and flew pigeons.

But 'the onerous duty' of his job began to tell on him and he confided in close friends that at least six of the people he had hanged he believed to be innocent. This belief played upon his conscience and his health. He resigned his post in 1892, aged 40, published his memoirs and loaned the rope that had been used in the attempted hanging of Lee to the Chamber of Horrors exhibit at Madame Tussauds in London. He became a committed Christian, in 1894 becoming an Evangelist preacher at the Bowland Street Mission in Bradford, and he remained a strong campaigner against capital punishment for the rest of his life.

Berry was a perfectionist and meticulous in his preparation for an execution – which his memoir shows – something that made the failure of the trap to work in Lee's case even more of a mystery. These are Berry's own words:

> It is, of course, necessary that the drop should be of sufficient length to cause instantaneous death, that is to say, to cause death by dislocation rather than by strangulation. Generally seven to ten feet. The rope I use is made of the finest Italian hemp, I adjust it just behind the left ear. The essential parts (of the scaffold) are few. There is a heavy cross-beam, into which bolts terminating in hooks (for the ropes) are fastened. (There are) two massive oaken doors, fixed in an oak frame-work on a level with the floor, and over a deep bricked pit. The first door is hung on three strong hinges, which are continued under the second. When the trap is set the ends of these long hinges rest on a draw-bar. When the lever is pulled over it moves the draw-bar in the opposite direction, so that the ends of the long hinges drop through the openings and the two doors fall.

So what went wrong at Exeter Prison? Berry produced this preliminary report for the authorities:

> Eight o'clock on Monday, 23 February 1885, was the time fixed for his execution. The scaffold and its arrangements had not been used for a previous execution, in their then position, though the drop had been used once, for the execution of Mrs. Took, but it was then fixed in another place. On the Saturday I examined this drop, and reported that it was much too frail for its purpose, but I worked the lever and found that the doors dropped all right. On the Monday morning, at the appointed time, I brought out the prisoner in the usual way, pinioned him and adjusted the noose. He was perfectly calm, almost indifferent. When the noose was adjusted I stood back and pulled over the lever.
>
> The noise of the bolts sliding could be plainly heard, but the doors did not fall. I stamped on the drop, to shake it loose, and so did some of the warders, but none of our efforts could stir it. Lee stood like a statue, making no sound or sign. As soon as we found our efforts useless we led the condemned man away. We tried the doors, which fell easily; then Lee was placed in position again, and again the doors refused to fall. Lee was led away, the doors tested for the third time (after wood was planed from the edges of both doors) – but again, to no avail.

At the time various theories were advanced for the failure of the workings, most popular being that it was caused by the doors being swollen with the rain that fell on the Sunday night. Berry concluded:

> That this was not the cause is proved, firstly, by the fact that the doors fell all right when the weight of the prisoner was not on them, and secondly, by the fact that they would not fall with the prisoner on them, even when we had chopped and planed down the sides where it was supposed that they stuck.

What then of Lee? John Lee served twenty-two years in prison, and was released in 1907 in a flurry of newspaper reports and magazine articles. He began his reintroduction into society by being photographed shaking hands with the vicar of Abbotskerswell. There began a small industry devoted to the production of articles, pamphlets, books and, later, plays, films and nowadays websites, devoted to mulling over the evidence and theorising over what might have been. He toured pubs and public halls recounting his story. A play was written about him and subsequently two films were produced under the title *The Man They Could Not Hang*. He married a girl from Newton Abbot in 1909 but later abandoned her. He left Britain in 1911 bound for a new life in America, where, during the Depression, he found employment as a shipping clerk for a trucking company. After a couple of changes of his first name – coincidentally perhaps to that of the man who tried to hang him – John Lee was buried in Milwaukee under the name 'James' Lee, having died of a heart attack in 1945, aged 80.

So who did murder Emma Keyse? The *Illustrated Police News*, in covering the original story, depicted sketches of the main characters on its front page for the benefit of its readers and here the artist may have inadvertently captured the likeness of the true killer. Reginald Gwynne Templar was a young solicitor who stepped forward – unasked and unexpectedly – on the morning of the discovery of the body and offered to act as the defence for Lee. There is speculation that he was the lover of Elizabeth Harris, the cook, and was, according to Lee at least, present in the house on the night of the murder. Two days into the trial, however, Templar was taken ill and died in December 1886 from 'paralysis of the insane' – a polite medical euphemism used at the time for a condition associated with tertiary syphilis. Was he the killer and Lee an accomplice – or was Lee, as he always maintained, innocent of the charge?

Capital punishment for murder in the UK was abolished in 1965 in Great Britain and 1973 in Northern Ireland. A YouGov poll in August 2014 showed that fewer than half of respondents would support reintroduction of the death penalty in the UK for murder. Of almost 2,000 people questioned, 45 per cent were in favour.

A chilling account of the West Country's greatest unsolved mystery.

THE DEVIL'S HOOF-PRINTS

Someone or something 'with cloven hooves' travelled silently across south and east Devon on a bitterly cold February night in 1855 and left its prints in the snow in a hundred-mile trail.

Who or what it was remains a mystery to this day but theories abound: these include suggestions that the tracks were made by a donkey, a kangaroo, an ape, various small animals including badgers, rabbits, hares, birds (with cloven hooves?), a team of practical jokers, some kind of natural electrical phenomena (as yet unknown), a meteorological balloon trailing a weighted lanyard, mass hysteria, a sea monster, a laser measuring device beamed down from a UFO, 400 Romanies on stilts – not to mention Old Nick himself.

But before getting totally side-tracked, perhaps it might be best to start with *The Times* of London, which printed this first account of this great mystery in its issue of 16 February 1855:

> Considerable sensation has been evoked in the towns of Topsham, Lympstone, Exmouth, Teignmouth, and Dawlish, in the south of

Devon, in consequence of the discovery of a vast number of foot tracks of a most strange and mysterious description. The superstitious go so far as to believe that they are the marks of Satan himself; and that great excitement has been produced among all classes may be judged from the fact that the subject has been descanted on from the pulpit. It appears that on Thursday night last there was a very heavy fall of snow in the neighbourhoods of Exeter and the south of Devon. On the following morning, the inhabitants of the above towns were surprised at discovering the tracks of some strange and mysterious animal, endowed with the power of ubiquity, as the foot prints were to be seen in all kinds of inaccessible places – on the tops of houses and narrow walls, in gardens and courtyards enclosed by high walls and palings, as well as in open fields. There was hardly a garden in Lympstone where the footprints were not observed.

The creature seems to have approached the doors of several houses and then to have retreated, but no one has been able to discover the standing or resting point of this mysterious visitor. On Sunday last the Rev. Mr. (G.M.) Musgrave (the vicar of Withycombe Raleigh) alluded to the subject in his sermon, and suggested the possibility of the footprints being those of a kangaroo,; but this could scarcely have been the case, as they were found on both sides of the estuary of the Exe. At present it remains a mystery, and many superstitious people in the above towns are actually afraid to go outside their doors after night.

Many years later, letters sent at the time to the *Illustrated London News* by the above mentioned reverend gentleman – and marked by him 'not for publication' – revealed that he had not believed a word of the escaped kangaroo story but had repeated it because so many of his parishioners believed this to be a supernatural occurrence. What we do have to thank him for are his drawings of the footprints, which accompanied his letter and which were published – anonymously.

Another correspondent with the *ILN* was a young man called William D'Urban of Countess Wear, Exeter, who was later to become the curator of the Royal Albert Memorial Museum in Exeter. He had spent time in Canada and was an experienced tracker of animals in the snow. By his own account he followed the Devon tracks for some miles through several parishes, and records that both the size and the distance between the footprints were uniform. He measured them as being 8½in long and said that they ran in a straight line. He also pointed out that although the change in temperature would cause the snow to melt and the track to enlarge as a consequence, this would be perfectly obvious to the observer, who would also clearly see the tracks of other known animals in the immediate area. The prints he took the trouble to track, measure and describe were unknown to him.

Others added to the general aura of mystery by claiming that when the track met an obstacle, like a wall or a building or even a haystack, it would stop on one side and start again on the other as though whatever it was had leapt over the obstacle. Later reports even talked of the track stopping on one side of the 2-mile-wide Exe estuary and then starting off again on the other. This was true but there is no evidence that anyone actually followed the same track across the thin ice. Just as chillingly perhaps is the recollection of another reverend, this time J.J. Rowe of Marychurch, Torquay, who said that he knew of a hunt that had followed the tracks for some distance and into a wood, at which point the hounds suddenly came tearing out again, 'baying and terrified'.

One hundred miles in a single night? Surely this was the work of more than one – whatever? A contemporary commentator on the mystery (and talking about one particular stretch of tracks) pointed out that 'to cross 40 miles, supposing steady progress and a generous 14 hours of darkness, with the generally reported stride of eight inches would require the perpetrator to move at the rate of six steps per second'. But several accounts make it clear that the trail was broken at a number of places. Another clerical gentleman, the Reverend H.T. Ellacombe, who came to Exmouth a few years after the event, was told by his parishioners that 'there were marks in the middle of a field, insulated – without any apparent approach or retreat'. Also in Exmouth a W. Courthope Forman said, 'The footprints came up the front garden to within a few feet of the house, stopped abruptly and began again at the back within a few feet of the building.'

Birds seem to be the most likely candidates in much of this and there were lengthy exchanges on the subject in both local and national newspapers. There had been foul weather along the east and south coasts several days earlier and large numbers of birds had come ashore from the Continent. But these being either web-footed or clawed, the question remained over what kinds of bird leave footprints 'like a donkey hoof' or 'closely resembling a donkey's shoe' as witnesses observed.

Small donkeys then remained prime suspects, especially since they tend to plant their feet in an almost perfect single line. But quite how they had managed to get into fenced gardens, leap barns and haystacks or balance along walls was never satisfactorily explained. Badgers attracted a lot of attention. They are nocturnal and can cover long distances in search of food – but a badger's prints are staggered and show both their pads and claws in the imprints. Next?

Kangaroos were favourite for a while. Two were kept in a private menagerie in Sidmouth owned by a Mr Fische and one of these had escaped, reported the *Exeter Flying Post*. But kangaroos cannot jump 14ft and leave a totally different track when they do finally land. Anyway, the story later turned out to be untrue when Mr Fische declared that neither of his kangaroos had escaped and could certainly vouch for their continued incarceration on the night in question.

Hot air or not, there was the balloon story, of course, but this came later. It was claimed by some that the Navy at Plymouth had released 'a top-secret weather balloon' from Devonport and were keeping quiet about it. What had happened, claimed the proponents of this particular bit of intelligence, was that its handlers had somehow lost control of it and it had moved eastwards during the hours of darkness, trailing a line beneath it to which was attached an iron weight of some kind that left its mark in the snow.

Gypsies was one of the more novel claims, made as late as 1973 by one Manfri Wood in his book *In the Life of a Romany Gypsy*. He wrote that the whole thing took eighteen months to plan and was the work of 400 gypsies from seven Romany tribes. They walked across the snows on 400 pairs of specially prepared 'measuring-stilts', he said. Their purpose was to scare away what he called 'rival tribes of Didekais and Pikies' – 'pagans all' – who were fervent believers in the Devil and had eyes on moving into the West Country.

But a very real fear among many of the common folk of rural Devon was that the notorious Spring-Heeled Jack had left London and was now roaming the narrow lanes of the county and ready 'come dimpsey' to pounce on any poor soul as was stupid enough to unbolt their doors and venture out into the dark. Spring-Heeled Jack was probably more than an urban myth in early and mid-Victorian Britain. He was never caught and there were probably several of them, half-baked mischief-makers all, in various parts of the country, who read the newspaper stories and set up their own franchises, copying each other. Many newspaper reports (the first in 1837) contain descriptions of his bizarre appearance – tall, skinny, dressed as the Devil and with sharp claws 'and eyes like red balls of fire'. His forte was to leap out of the darkness on to a hapless victim (usually female) in a lonely place, to tear at their clothing and faces with steel-like claws before leaping away again into the blackness of the night. This ability to make enormous jumps gave him his nickname. Spring-Heeled Jack's activities diminished as the century wore on but his memory was kept alive in many of the best-selling penny dreadfuls of the day. Warnings to the young to be home before dark 'else Spring-Heeled Jack'll get you!' lasted well into the Edwardian era, and not only in the West.

The most likely answer is that there is probably no single explanation. The 'hoof-prints' in the snow were, like as not, made by animals or birds or both. Sometimes even, as the stories of the Devil got around, by mischief-makers out to torment their neighbours. Until a solution is found, the story of the Devil's hoof-prints is probably best filed away alongside crop circles, the Bermuda Triangle, the Loch Ness Monster and maybe even things that go bump in the night.

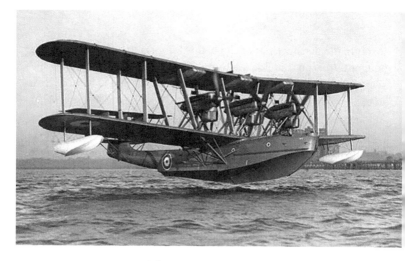

'These were my golden years.'

LAWRENCE OF ARABIA IN DEVON

By the time Lawrence managed to cut himself free from all ties of the Great War and its long drawn-out aftermath of diplomatic negotiations and treaties, it was 1921 and he was physically and emotionally exhausted.

It was time, at last, for Colonel Thomas Edward Lawrence, legendary hero of the 1916–18 Sinai and Palestine Campaign and the Arab Revolt against the Ottoman Turks, to 'disappear' from public view. Only a handful of intimate friends (including Winston Churchill) knew of his plan to escape the limelight completely by walking into a recruiting office in Covent Garden to join the Royal Air Force under an assumed name. He emerged as 352087 A/c John Hume Ross. He later wrote: 'Airmen have few possessions, few ties, little daily care. For me, duty now orders only the brightness of these five buttons down my front.' Alas, the career of A/c Ross – detailed in his book *The Mint* – was short-lived and came to an abrupt end after a few months when he was unmasked by the press and again hounded for interviews, opinions and job offers. He said: 'To have news value is to have a tin can tied to one's tail.'

But with friends in high places he went still deeper under cover and in 1923 changed his name again, this time to T.E. Shaw, and joined the Royal Tank Corps as a private. He once claimed he had picked the name Shaw from a telephone directory but George Bernard Shaw was a close friend and had given Lawrence his first Brough motorcycle – so believe that as you may. In the RTC he was dubbed 'Broughie'. He welcomed this second escape, hated his life in khaki but loved Dorset, where he was stationed, making friends with Thomas Hardy and leasing a tumble-down cottage called Clouds Hill from cousins who lived near Bovington Camp. After much string-pulling, he was able to leave the army and was finally readmitted to the RAF again in 1925. He went to India and Afghanistan but 1929 found him back in England once more, this time as an engineer and stationed in Devon, at RAF Cattewater, later to become RAF Mount Batten, Plymouth, a seaplane station.

He had a great fondness for Devon, especially Dartmoor, which he crossed and recrossed many times on his Brough. From Mount Batten he continued to write and translate books and to resume his many friendships with artists, politicians and other writers. He also became the right-hand man of his commanding officer, Wing Commander Sydney Smith, and his wife, during the preparations for the international Schneider Trophy seaplane race over the Solent. At Mount Batten he joined a team working on the development of high-speed rescue craft for downed aircrew. He was working alongside a man he knew well, Hubert Scott-Paine, a motorboat racer and the designer of the boats that had captured the world water-speed record at nearly 100mph. Lawrence had witnessed the crash of a seaplane on the Solent and had been 'mortified' by the slowness of the seaplane tender sent to the rescue. Designed simply as a vessel to transfer fuel and supplies, it was completely unsuited to the task and the pilot drowned. He later wrote: 'When I went into RAF boats in 1929, every type was an Admiralty design. All were round-bottomed, derived from the first hollow tree, with only a fin, called a keel, to delay their rolling about and over. They progressed by pushing their own bulk of water aside.' Lawrence worked tirelessly for the rest of his career in the RAF to persuade the service to adopt purpose-built fast rescue vessels. The 200-class and Mk I seaplane tender gave the RAF its first rapid-response air-sea rescue capability and evolved to become the high-speed rescue launches developed for the RAF that were to save countless lives during the Second World War.

During periods of leave and at weekends it was his great joy to travel between Clouds Hill, near Wimborne, to Plymouth along the winding coast road on his beloved Brough Superior: he loved the power and speed of these 1,000cc machines and owned eight of them during his short lifetime. It seems he enjoyed a very privileged existence at Mount Batten, where his true identity was kept a well-guarded secret among the principals at the station. One of his contemporaries recalled: 'The buttons on Shaw's working tunic were a brilliant shade of green: he never attended any parades; in fact, he pleased himself about most things.'

Came late morning on Wednesday, 4 February 1931 and Lawrence was sitting on a bench just below the Martello Tower overlooking Plymouth Sound, drinking coffee from a flask and chatting. In spite of the month, it was a warm spring day, no wind and the water calm. With him was Clare Sydney Smith, who had joined him for 'elevenses'. The seaplane they were watching was flying low across the water towards them, on a training exercise and flying at about 70mph when it suddenly nose-dived. The aircraft was a Blackburn Iris Mk III, an experimental aircraft and the largest in the RAF at that time. What they were about to witness was the worst disaster in the history of aviation until that date.

An eyewitness to the crash later told the inquiry: 'We watched it flying towards Mount Batten when suddenly it struck the water, nose first, turned turtle, then over on its side. It seemed the petrol tank had burst, as there was a lot of petrol running out but there was no explosion and we saw no smoke or flame.'

Lawrence scrambled down to the water's edge and he and his commanding officer jumped into a motorboat and were quickly on the scene. The duty boat was already there and had pulled two men on board. Ten others were still inside the aircraft. A small coastal trawler was able to drag a line under part of the hull and brought it nearer to the surface, its distinctive tail section swaying in the air. Immediately Lawrence 'became master of the situation', stripped off his overalls and with others began a series of deep dives down and inside the fuselage of the aircraft in an attempt to find anyone who might still be alive in an air pocket in the upturned hull. He must have been in great pain. He had sustained an injury in an earlier air crash when he had been the sole survivor: 'My breathing hurt me. After the Handley crash in Rome the X-ray showed one rib furred like the bristles of a toothbrush, against the wall of my chest; and much lung-pumping taps its thin dagger-pain into my heart.'

Two more lives were saved, though one died later from his injuries. Eight of the twelve people on board perished in the crash and six bodies were never recovered: two of the crew are buried at Ford Park Cemetery. Someone who was stationed there at the time, George Foden, later wrote:

> Lawrence supported one survivor who was in a bad way, until he could be lifted from the water and rushed to hospital. A photographer managed to get on board one of the salvage boats where Shaw was working, and at last got him into his view-finder. Shaw rounded on him like a caged animal, tore the camera from his hands and pushed him over the side and into the very cold water. As he surfaced, Shaw threw the camera at him, which bounced off and disappeared beneath the waves.

At the subsequent Air Ministry Court of Inquiry, Colonel T.E. Lawrence, *aka* Leading Aircraftsman Shaw, made known his opinion of where the blame lay for the crash: pilot error. Wing Commander C.G. Tucker, who was at the controls, had pulled rank and retained control in the landing of the plane over the pilot, Flight Lieutenant M.H. Ely, who was far more experienced. Tucker was killed in the crash, Ely survived to give evidence 'from a hospital couch and too weak to hold the Bible'. At the public inquest the newspapers, now aware of the true identity of the 5ft 5in aircraftsman in court, made much of Lawrence's part in the proceedings, but still referred to him as Shaw. The *Western Weekly News* of 21 February reported:

> An important witness was Aircraftsman Edward Shaw ... a short, compact figure, in the neat, well-fitting uniform of the service, with his buttons highly polished, Aircraftsman Shaw, punctiliously adding 'Sir' to all his replies. Asked did he do any flying, he replied, 'No, but I used to, sir.' He also stated that if ordered to fly with that pilot he would have done so, 'but not from choice', he added.

There was to be another Iris flying boat crash at Mount Batten early in 1933. Again Lawrence was on the spot and this time was able to speed out to the rescue in one of the new and faster power boats he had helped to design and build. He left the service 'reluctantly' in 1935, calling them 'my golden years'. At that time he had been stationed at the Marine and Armament Experimental Establishment at RAF Felixstowe, where he supervised the armour-plating of diesel-powered launches that were to be used for RAF bombing practice. His growing mood of despondency had increased as his discharge from the RAF grew nearer and the final removal of his 'blue covering', as he called it. He wrote: 'My looming discharge from the Air Force makes me low-toned. It is like a hermit-crab losing his twelve-year-old shell.'

It was on 26 February 1935 that Lawrence received his discharge from the RAF and, wearing tweed jacket and flannels, and with a knapsack on his back containing little more than a clean shirt and his shaving tackle, set off from RAF Bridlington for Clouds Hill, Dorset, on a push bike, making 60–70 miles a day. On the way he called in at Chartwell, Kent, the home of Winston Churchill, who recalled:

> The last time he came was a few weeks before his death. He was riding only a 'push-bike'! He was going, he told me, to get rid of his motorcycle. He could not afford such luxuries. I reminded him that he had the purse of Fortunatus. He had but to lift his hand. But he tossed his head disdainfully. Such a thing as a motorcycle was beyond his means. Alas, he did not stick to this opinion!

It was only a few weeks later that Lawrence was fatally injured when his motorcycle left the road near his cottage at Clouds Hill, a scene dramatically recreated in the opening sequence of the 1962 film *Lawrence of Arabia*, with Peter O'Toole in the title role.

With that image in many people's minds, this seems a good place to set the record straight on the so-called 'assassination' theories and the 'mysterious black car' seen at about the time of the accident. Many a good yarn has been spun on the strength of this 'mystery' but the facts are not at all mysterious. One of Lawrence's cronies was Henry Williamson the author, probably best-known for his book *Tarka the Otter*. He lived in north Devon and had written to Lawrence at Clouds Hill on Saturday, 11 March asking could he motor down to see him on Tuesday 14 March to discuss a manuscript. Although they had corresponded over several years, they had only met twice before and Williamson had not been to Clouds Hill before. Lawrence received the letter on the Monday morning – the morning of the accident – and rode his motorbike to Bovington Camp post office to send Williamson the following thirteen-word telegram:

11.25 BOVINGTON CAMP. WILLIAMSON + SHALLOWFORD + FILLEIGH + LUNCH TUESDAY WET + FIND COTTAGE 1 MILE NORTH BOVINGTON CAMP + SHAW.

On the return journey to the cottage he crested a hill and swerved to avoid two boys on bicycles in the hidden dip on the other side. He lost control and went over the handlebars. The police estimated that his machine had been travelling at almost full speed when it left the road – which for a Brough Superior was 97mph. He died six days later, an hour before sunrise, on Sunday, 19 May 1935, without gaining consciousness. He was 46 years old. A few days earlier he had written to an artist friend, Eric Kenington:

You wonder what I am doing? Well, so do I, in truth. Days seem to dawn, suns to shine, evenings to follow, and then I sleep. What I have done, what I am doing, what I am going to do, puzzle and bewilder me. Have you ever been a leaf and fallen from your tree in autumn and been really puzzled about it? That's the feeling.

He was buried, his body wrapped in the Union Flag, in a small rectangular plot opposite the churchyard of St Nicholas's Church, Moreton, Dorset. His cottage at Clouds Hill can be visited and is in the care of the National Trust.

Was this the Poet Laureate's favourite seaside town?

HOW SIDMOUTH INSPIRED BETJEMAN

It was the summer of '62 and John Betjeman arrived in Sidmouth, complete with suitcase, fountain pen and camera crew, to make a film about the East Devon town for Television Wales & the West (TWW) or 'good old Tellywelly' as Betjeman liked to call the company that later became HTV.

With him during that stay was Jonathan Stedall (who went on to become a renowned independent documentary film maker, but was then a 23-year-old director given his first major television assignment to work alongside the man later to become poet laureate) to produce a series of documentaries on places of Betjeman's choosing in the West Country. It was the start of a friendship that was to last until the great man's death, in 1984: it was also the first time that Betjeman had ever written a script in rhyme.

'Our brief was to create portraits of places which were close to Betjeman's heart,' Jonathan Stedall recalls in his introduction to the book of the film, *Still Sidmouth*. 'Sidmouth was, I believe, the first place we visited together', although why Betjeman chose the town for the first of his twelve locations or why he decided to immortalise it in poetry, no one is sure. What is known is that he wrote two other television scripts in elegant rhyming couplets, one on Marlborough, his old school, which he loathed, the other on the Victorian engineer Brunel, whom he greatly admired. But neither subject allowed the poet the lightness of touch he employed in his masterful sketch of what now stands revealed perhaps as his favourite seaside town.

Broad crescents basking in the summer sun,
A sense of sea and holidays begun,
Leisure to live and breathe and smell and look:
Unfold for me this seaside history book.

He worked closely with Stedall during the planning of the film and spent three days at a seafront hotel, discussing what might be included. But, as with all their work together, Betjeman waited until he was invited to the cutting room to view the first edit of the film before writing the script to picture. Then he took out his fountain pen and wrote *Still Sidmouth* in rhyme, in a single sitting, astounding everybody. 'One of Betjeman's outstanding qualities was his kindness and I think this shows in his script,' Stedall said. 'A lot of his observations are very personal. He imagines, for example, what people might be saying to one another or what they might be thinking. But he is never cruel. Fundamentally he loved life and people.'

As Stedall's discreet camera follows two women, strolling to the town's narrow shopping streets, Betjeman pictures their conversation:

Clocks in a hundred houses all chime three:
It's time to saunter to the town for tea
To exercise the dog and have a chat
On this and this and this and that and that.

'Two and eleven? My goodness what a price!
Now don't go there, dear; do take my advice.'
'Oh, everything is dearer now, I fear.
Do you find dear things so much dearer, dear?'

Betjeman certainly knew the town well and was undoubtedly attracted by its architecture. But Sidmouth has many charms, not least of which is its location. Sidmouth is little changed since the film was made, except (as elsewhere) for traffic, which Betjeman hated. Admittedly, the butchers with its polished brass shop front became a bistro, and the old-fashioned oil shop went on to sell gifts and reproduction furniture, but Sidmouth is still Sidmouth, its character remains intact and the fabric of the place is much as Betjeman saw it:

> Mansions for admirals by the pebbly strand;
> And cottages for maiden aunts inland
> That go with tea and strawberries and cream.
> Sweet sheltered gardens by the twisting stream:
> Cob, thatch and fuchsia bells, a Devon dream.

Betjeman's genius for words and their effortless delivery perfectly complemented Stedall's style of film making. During twenty-two years they produced many memorable programmes together, including famously, *Summoned by Bells* and *Thank God it's Sunday*.

Shortly before the poet laureate's final illness and his consequent retreat from public life, Stedall stepped unobtrusively in front of the camera to lead Betjeman back through many memories of his life to produce the autobiographical *Time with Betjeman*. Near the end of that final programme, sitting in the morning sun on his porch in Cornwall, a travel rug about his knees, he was asked whether he had any regrets. With a twinkle in his eye he answered quietly, 'Yes, I haven't had enough sex'.

He died at Trebetherick, Cornwall, in May 1984 after a long illness, with Stedall one of the six pall-bearers at the funeral. They carried Betjeman's coffin through driving rain across a mile of countryside to St Enodoc's churchyard where he is buried. 'It was,' Stedall recalls, 'as though the elements themselves were celebrating his extraordinary life.'

The 178 lines of classic Betjeman in the *Still Sidmouth* script provide a glimpse of his gentle and sometimes mischievous sense of fun that endeared him to millions of readers and viewers, as the last but one line of the poem reveals:

> Farewell, seductive Sidmouth by the sea,
> Older and more exclusive than Torquay,
> Sidmouth in Devon, you're the town for me!

CORNWALL

Where would Cornwall be without King Arthur?

LAND OF MYTH AND LEGEND

Never discuss politics or religion in a pub is good advice to anyone, anywhere – save for Cornwall – where it might be wise to add 'or King Arthur'.

For though dyed-in-the-wool historians raise scholarly eyebrows at so many of Cornwall's Arthurian yarns along with tales of mermaids, piskies, tin mine 'knockers', headless horsemen and ghostly galleons, for the county's 4½ million annual visitors it is all very much part of the charm of the place as well as grist to the mill for a thriving tourism industry.

But what follows – for the most part – is neither myth nor legend but simply a selection and retelling of real people, places and events that have made Cornwall the extraordinarily wonderful and unique place it has become and will always be.

There is a vanished realm beneath the waves off Land's End …

IN AT THE DEEP END

Buy a Cornish fisherman a pint and he will wave his arm towards the sea and tell you that long ago there was a land out there called Lyonnesse. It was swallowed up by the ocean in a single night, he'll tell you, and only one man escaped to tell the tale. A second pint and a pasty perhaps will reveal that the Seven Stones reef yonder (some 18 miles west of Land's End) is the top-most pinnacle of King Arthur's Camelot.

In the same vein, a time-traveller buying an Ancient Greek fisherman a flask of wine and a slab of moussaka would have been told a different tale, less vague than the Cornish yarn but much nearer the truth. He too would have begun by waving his arm towards the sea but then continued by telling you that there was once a Greek called Pytheas, a geographer and explorer, who sailed from what is nowadays Marseilles on a peaceful voyage of discovery to northern Europe. Knowledge of Gaul and Britain had already reached the Mediterranean but it was of the foggiest kind. This was 325 BCE. Pytheas was real enough and almost certainly circumnavigated Britain, and on his travels came across 'The Tin Islands'. The Greeks knew about them from traders from the Eastern

Mediterranean, who as early as the ninth century BCE traded wine for tin but kept quiet about its location. The Greek word for tin, he would have reminded you, is *cassiteros*: it occurs in Homer and is thought to have been of Celtic origin. The Phoenicians traded wine and saffron for tin. Nearly 3,000 years later the Cornish are famed for their saffron cakes.

If you were still looking doubtful he would have reminded you that the Cassiterides or Tin Islands is also recorded by another Greek, this time the historian Herodotus in 445 BCE, who tells us that those secretive traders spoke of them as being two separate islands. That is the Cornwall peninsula as it was once perceived, and what we now nowadays call the Scillies or, once-upon-a-time, 'Lyonnesse' perhaps?

Being dubbed romantically – but wrongly – as 'Lyonnesse' since the early Middle Ages (more of which anon) has caused it to be tarred with the same brush as today's trade in piskies, giants and ghostly galleons. That other 'island', of course, remains as a place that touches the spirit of all who travel, venture or settle there. That place is forever Cornwall, as real and wonderful today as it ever was.

Daphne du Maurier, in the opening paragraph of her book *Vanishing Cornwall*, was deeply touched by this extraordinary sense of place when she wrote that here was the freedom she desired 'to write, to walk, to wander, freedom to climb hills, to pull a boat, to be alone. I for this, and this for me.' Tennyson, Thomas Hardy, Walter de la Mare, Sylvia Plath and Swinburne all wrote poems about Lyonnesse, the latter being 'Tristram of Lyonnesse', an epic poem set in Arthurian times that retells the story of the ill-fated lovers Tristram and Yseult. The only fault with Swinburne's retelling, however, must be laid at the door of the highly imaginative early French troubadours – from whence it came – without them bothering to tie down the actual location too precisely in their lyrics. Unwittingly they planted the seeds of confusion when they sang and wrote about a real place called Léonois, which is the Latin name for Lothian, in Scotland. Subsequent continental writers and reciters of Arthurian romances decided that Lyonnesse (as it had now become) was better to be found in Cornwall – which they and their audiences had heard of – rather than Lothian, which they had not.

Although no mention of a drowned land is made in any Arthurian legend, nothing was allowed to stand in the way of a good yarn and the capital of Lyonnesse came into being as the 'City of Lions'. Neither has the actual Cornish name for this lost land anything to do with its sinking. It is Lethowsow. It translates as 'the milky ones' because of the white water surrounding the Seven Stones reef and was not used until well into the reign of Good Queen Bess. Full steam ahead to 1852, when the Great Western Railway extended its line to Penzance and in pursuit of ticket sales chose to graft a little meat on to the bones of the legend in its promotional literature. They gave a precise date to what we would nowadays call a tsunami. It came about, the GWR said, at dusk on 11 November 1099. Quite where that small gem of information came from is anybody's guess although Mount's Bay was certainly inundated by a sea flood in 1044 and several villages and many people were drowned. But for the record, the fable says that the one man who escaped the flood – whenever it was – was a farmer, an ancestor of the old Cornish family of Trevelyan. He had foreseen what might be coming and had moved his family from his Lyonnesse estate and was making one final stock check when the sea broke in upon it. Thanks to his trusty steed, Trevelyan made it to dry land at Perranuthnoe, which is just round the corner from Land's End in Mount's Bay.

This part of Cornwall has always attracted creative people, dreamers, imaginative souls, drawn by the quality of the light – which is extraordinary – the landscape and the frequent changes in the sea and the weather. Painters, poets, writers and photographers especially are drawn to the end of the land, bound perhaps for the onward journey to the Scillies and forever in search of the spirit of place. Witness September 1860, when the painters Holman Hunt and Valentine Cameron Prinsep packed paints and palettes at Paddington and headed for the dazzling sunlight and balmy breezes of Penzance. Here they crossed to the Scillies, some 37 miles distant, to join the great man himself, Alfred Lord Tennyson, who was beginning another of his several walking tours of his beloved Cornwall.

'After a day spent in visiting the gardens of the Scilly Isles,' Hunt wrote, 'we returned to Penzance. During the intercourse of this journey we were much engaged in discussions on the character of English poetry of all periods ... Tennyson in his slouch hat, his rusty black suit, and his clinging coat, wandering away among the rocks' – where he later slipped and sprained his ankle and spent the rest of his walking tour in a pony and trap. But was a day really enough even for two painters to gather anything other than a fleeting impression of the Scillies? A fellow Victorian, Walter Besant, had something to say on the subject in his novel *Armorel of Lyonesse* (1884):

> The visitor who comes by one boat and goes away by the next thinks he has seen this archipelago. As well stand inside a cathedral for half an hour and then go away thinking you have seen all. It takes many days to see these fragments of Lyonnesse and to get a true sense of the place.

Another poet, Palgrave, who published his Golden Treasury the following year, joined the party and was so overwhelmed to be in the company of the poet laureate that he dedicated the work to Tennyson, whose 'encouragement, given while traversing the wild scenery of Treryn Dinas led me to begin the work'. Treryn Dinas is a headland near Treen, on the Penwith Peninsula between Penberth Cove and Porthcurno. It is spectacularly beautiful and the site of an Iron Age promontory fort that Tennyson knew well and found a magical place to write. Tennyson and his Cornish muse perpetuated the myth of the land destined to vanish beneath the waves in 'The Idylls of the King', in the iambic pentameter no less, that extraordinarily noble rhythm much loved by teachers of English literature. Lyonnesse, mused Tennyson, was the site of the final battle between Arthur and Mordred.

> Then rose the King and moved his host by night
> And ever pushed Sir Mordred, league by league,
> Back to the sunset bound of Lyonnesse –
> A land of old upheaven from the abyss
> By fire, to sink into the abyss again;
> Where fragments of forgotten peoples dwelt,
> And the long mountains ended in a coast
> Of ever-shifting sand, and far away
> The phantom circle of a moaning sea.

'Upheaven from the abyss by fire', of course, is a poet's way of referring to the kind of cataclysmic submarine upheaval that we know triggers tsunamis, a series of waves that travel across the open ocean at great speeds and build into large deadly waves in the shallower water of a shoreline. There was a particularly devastating one recorded in the Bristol Channel on 30 January 1607. Some 200 square miles of low-lying land in Devon, Somerset, Gloucestershire and South Wales were flooded. More than 2,000 people were drowned and houses, villages and even churches were swept away.

Celtic mythology is full of tales of world-changing floods and there are Welsh legends of a drowned kingdom in Cardigan Bay. As long ago as the Bronze Age, sea levels rose and took over the land around the area of what is today's Mounts Bay, and the Cornish name for St Michael's Mount is Karrek Loos y'n Koos, which means 'the grey rock in the wood'. It may not come as a surprise therefore that at the time of extreme low tides there is evidence of a sunken forest in Mount's Bay when petrified tree stumps have been revealed. With such evidence the idea of Lyonnesse must surely begin to emerge as something a little more tangible than a fairy story?

In short, Lyonnesse – or whatever its name was – and whether it was overwhelmed in a night or a millennium, seems to be a survival of folk memory: and what credence, in this day and age, should one pay to folk memory? The best people to answer that probably are the Cornish people themselves, who will be happy to remind you that it is today what it always has been and will be tomorrow. Cornwall's folk memory is Truth in the robes of Poetry!

Few places in this ancient Celtic land are less than 20 miles from the sea, 10 from a holy place or seemingly an arm's length from a poet.

A REALM OF SAINTS AND POETS

Those Cornish who remind you of their old adage, 'There are more saints in Cornwall than in all of heaven' are surely exaggerating but since the Gospel was brought to Cornwall in the fifth century it became known, in ecclesiastical circles, as 'the land of saints'. It produced such numbers of holy men and women, hermits, ascetics, missionaries, abbots and holy bishops – not to mention holy springs, wells, rocks and caves – that just about every hamlet, village or town has its own patron saint.

Very little is known about most of them because written records were lost or destroyed at the Norman Conquest or after the Reformation. Precisely how many of them existed historically is also unknown but all of them have stories, legends and fables attached to them. But if you want to get by in Cornwall it helps that you should know a little about three of them. These are Piran and Petrock – both undoubtedly historically real flesh and blood holy men – and then there is also Michael, the archangel, as well as another saintly being – but we'll come to him later.

Saint Piran is the patron saint of tin-miners and the patron saint of Cornwall, although Saint Petroc and St Michael also have some claim to this title. Piran's flag is a white cross on a black background and came about, so the story goes, from Piran's rediscovery of tin smelting. Although tin had been traded with the Phoenicians, the tin-smelting process had been lost until, lo and behold, his black hearthstone (a slab of tin-bearing ore no less) had the tin smelt out of it and rise to the top in the form of a white cross. This happened, perhaps in Perranporth, where he first landed from Ireland and built a small oratory or chapel.

Saint Petroc has been called 'the captain of Cornish saints'. He was probably born in the second half of the fifth century in South Wales and was a son of a king. He was reportedly 'handsome, courteous in speech, prudent, modest, burning with unceasing love, always ready for all good works for the Church'. He studied in Ireland for twenty years, then sailed to Cornwall, where he was very active as a missionary and founded monasteries and churches throughout the south-west peninsula. On the homeward journey from a pilgrimage to Rome and the Holy Land with a party of followers, they got back as far as Devon when it began to rain heavily. Petroc told them that the morrow would dawn bright and dry. Alas when they awoke and found it still pouring with rain Petroc was so humbled by his pronouncement that instead of splashing onwards into Cornwall with them, he turned on his heel and trudged alone the thousand or so miles back to Rome again, as penance.

Petroc and Piran were both humble men and their chosen closeness to nature throughout their lives brought them to places of natural spiritual power as they sought and found the inner peace through which they could live and pray and preach. They found inspiration in Cornwall – as it continues to inspire so many people today – in both quiet contemplation as well as in the physical act of simply walking. 'Emotion recalled in tranquility' – as Wordsworth once described poetry – was also true for these ancient Cornish holy men and women as they spent long periods of time in mindful contemplation.

'Walking the straight and narrow' and being on the right track are metaphors for being on a journey leading to enlightenment. There are still short stretches of monastic paths and tracks across the moors in the West Country that helped travellers find their way between places. There are also some extraordinary 'pathways' that link holy places, much loved by today's New Age movement: intriguing, mysterious and as a consequence, controversial. Most famous and remarkable of these in Cornwall centres around St Michael, the Archangel and so-called ley lines or alignments. These are hypothetical alignments of a number of places such as ancient monuments and megaliths. One of these, called 'The Michael Line', runs in a straight line, west to east from St Michael's Mount via Glastonbury Tor, the Avebury Henge and onwards by leaps and bounds but straight as an arrow across the intervening miles to Bury St Edmunds Abbey, after which is disappears into the North Sea and is last seen heading towards what marine archaeologists today call Doggerland.

A second alignment, again perfectly straight, begins at a sixth-century monastery on the tiny rocky island of Skellig Michael, off the Iveragh Peninsula in County Kerry, Ireland, before crossing to Cornwall's St Michael's Mount, thence to Mont St Michel in Normandy before continuing its bee-line through Europe via seven sanctuaries dedicated to St Michael: although very far from each other they are perfectly aligned, with the three most important sites, Mont St Michel in France, the Sacra of San Miguel in Val de Susa and the Sanctuary of Monte Sant'Angelo in the Gargano, all the same distance from each other. The alignment finishes at Mount Carmel, in Israel.

Before there were smartphones and selfies, Cornish saints and poets alike *looked*; that is they looked *hard*, observed, listened, sniffed the air, felt the wind or the rain on their faces and remembered, experienced the totality of their surroundings before moving on. Later they talked about that experience or wrote it down. To quote Wordsworth again, 'I have said that poetry is the spontaneous overflow of powerful feelings: the emotion is contemplated until the tranquillity gradually disappears', and words – written or spoken – take over. Holy man, poet and eccentric, the Reverend Robert Stephen Hawker (1803–75) of Morwenstow wrote poetry that was very popular in the Victorian period. He famously wrote 'The Song of the Western Men' with the chorus, 'And shall Trelawny die? Here's twenty thousand Cornish men will know the reason why!' He was eccentric both in his clothes and his habits and the only black things he ever wore were his socks. Another cleric wrote of him, 'He dressed in claret-coloured coat, blue fisherman's jersey, long sea-boots, a pink brimless hat and a poncho made from a yellow horse blanket, which he claimed was the ancient habit of St Padarn. He talked to birds, invited his nine cats into church and kept a pig as a pet.'

He wrote much of his poetry in the small hut he built for himself from driftwood on the cliffs overlooking the Atlantic, where it remains as the smallest property in the National Trust portfolio. Shortly before his death he converted to Roman Catholicism and at his request the mourners at his funeral in Plymouth (where he had been born) all wore purple.

Cornwall inspired the poet Laurence Binyon, a Quaker, the son of a cleric and too old at 45 to be called up to fight in the trenches in the Great War. Instead he volunteered to be a stretcher-bearer at the front line, where he was greatly moved by the horrors of the conflict. Thus he is especially remembered as one of the leading war poets and for one poem in particular. He wrote it one late summer evening, sitting on the cliffs between Pentire Point and The Rumps. It is called 'For the Fallen' and the commemorative plaque at that place reproduces the fourth stanza:

They shall grow not old, as we that are left grow old
Age shall not weary them, nor the years condemn
At the going down of the sun and in the morning
We will remember them

Another famous poet forever associated with Cornwall and who so loved the place that he lived there in his latter years and wrote about it memorably in both prose and verse was John Betjeman. He is buried in St Enodoc's Church, to the south of Trebetherick on the north Cornwall coast, which is thought to be built on the site of a cave where St Enodoc the Hermit lived and baptised converts at the Jesus Well half a mile away. Some believe that Enodoch was in fact a woman named Qendydd who came from Wales and was a hermit during the sixth century. Little else is known about her, except that her feast day is on 7 March. The church can only be reached on foot, and when Betjeman's coffin was carried the half mile across the fairways of the local golf club one of his pall-bearers, the film director Jonathon Stedall, said 'The skies opened as though heaven itself was weeping for the day'.

Perhaps the best known of Cornish poets is Charles Causeley (1917–2003), who was born in Launceston and, although widely travelled, he lived most of his life there and always retained his native Cornish accent. He was also a writer, a broadcaster, a playwright and specially a writer of poetry and prose for children. He once said that all poetry is magic and wrote that it is 'a spell against insensitivity, failure of imagination, ignorance and barbarism'. He was very much a narrative poet and a poet of place, drawing inspiration from his native home.

John Harris (1820–84) was so poor as a child that he wrote his poetry on paper bags using blackberry juice for ink. He is perhaps the least known and yet most extraordinarily gifted of Cornish poets. He was a miner, poet and latterly a preacher. Born in the hamlet of Bolenowe, near Troon, south of Camborne, he was eldest of nine children and was sent to work at Dolcoath tin mine when he was 12. All of his poetry, be it about the toil of mining or in celebration of the landscapes and seascapes around Carn Brea, is strong and powerful and all of it was written, not at a table, but in the open air. He spent twenty years in the darkness of the mines and only left Cornwall once in his life, to briefly visit Stratford-upon-Avon to receive an award. When one of his poems, 'The First Primrose', was eventually published in a magazine, it attracted some attention, and was soon followed by a collection, published in 1853. Soon after this, he was able to leave mining forever to become a scripture reader in Falmouth. He became a Quaker and joined the Society of Friends at Falmouth in 1879 and was elected a Fellow of the Royal Historical Society. He went on to publish several volumes of poetry during his lifetime, including *A Story of Carn Brea*. This pagan hilltop from his childhood days was his special place. When he was dying in 1884, he asked to be buried at Treslothan Chapel at the foot of this hill, where his six-year-old daughter, Lucretia was laid to rest. Her eulogy is his most moving poem.

Harris, like those ancient Cornish holy men and women before him, was a good person who was also inspired. If there is poetry to be mined in any of us, Cornwall is surely the place to unearth it, to take home, hammer it into shape and eventually, if one feels so inclined, share it with others. It doesn't need to scan, it doesn't even need to rhyme. It only needs to be externalised. Written down. 'Emotions recollected in tranquility.'

Pirates were never gentlemen but once in a while they were ladies.

THE PIRATE QUEEN OF PENRYN

Like a spider waiting patiently at the edge of her web, Mary Killigrew spent long days at her chamber window high above the bay, looking for the fat foreign cargo vessels that would become her next kill.

A gentlewoman by birth, she was, by all accounts, 'a bad lot', a thrill seeker and only escaped hanging thanks to the massive bribe paid to Queen Elizabeth I by her equally wicked husband.

With her father, Philip Wolverton, described as 'a gentleman pirate' of Wolverston Hall in Suffolk, it is perhaps not surprising that piracy flowed in Mary's veins. Widowed young of her husband Henry Knyvett, she wandered west, where she found the pickings richer and easier to come by when she married again. This time it was into the ancient Cornish family of Killigrew (it took its name from Killigrew in the parish of Saint Erme), who also happened to be in the same line of business.

Thus it was that Mary Knyvett, widowed pirate's daughter, was transformed into Lady Mary Killigrew of Arwenack Hall, near Penryn, pirate extraordinary and receiver of stolen goods, cattle and what have you.

The man she married was Sir John Killigrew, another bad lot but also Captain in Command of Pendennis Castle. Here he seemed to lead something of a charmed life until one remembers that both he and his father had been staunch opponents of the Catholic queen 'Bloody' Mary and were imprisoned for it. When Elizabeth came to the throne she smiled favourably on the Killigrews and they returned to royal favour and Killigrew's father to his role as Pendennis Castle's first captain.

The governorship of the castle allowed the Killigrews control of all of the shipping in the Carrick Roads Harbour and along part of the south coast. Thus empowered, all cargoes became their prey and within a short time John, the son, turned Arwenack House into a fortified stronghold to store their ill-gotten gains. Not only did Mary wallow in her new-found wealth, she is also reported to have revelled in the adventure that the capture and plunder of each vessel brought about.

Came New Year's Day, January 1583 and a Spanish galleon, *The Marie Saint Sebastian*, sheltering from a storm, had the misfortune to drop anchor in Falmouth Harbour, under the ever-watchful eye of Mary, whose custom it was to sit in an upper chamber of Arwenack House, watching the comings and goings of foreign vessels. This heavily laden 144-ton ship was clearly a heaven-sent prize to launch a new year of thievery. She watched two men row themselves ashore. Both were merchants: John de Chavis and Philip de Oryo, who was also the captain. The ship remained at anchor for several days, awaiting a wind, and this gave her time to plan. In her husband's absence at Pendennis Castle, she plotted to rob the ship after having first induced the two merchants to leave their inn at Penryn and re-join their ship so that all of them could be despatched in one fell swoop. In this she was to be unsuccessful – something she was to live to regret – but her wicked scheme was played out.

At midnight on 7 January a boatload of her ruffians boarded the galleon, the crew was butchered and their bodies thrown overboard. They then upped anchor, slipped out of the harbour and set sail for Ireland to dispose of the loot, as well as the ship. But before they made sail, it was arranged that two of Lady Killigrew's servants were sent back with the boat carrying her share. Kendal and Hawkins were their names and the bolts of cloth and bundles of fine leather they deposited on the floor of the great hall at Arwenack as her share did not please her. In fact, she was so incensed not to be looking upon the treasure it had been rumoured would be coming her way, that she resolved that her kinswoman, Mrs Killigrew, and the maids and servants in the house would receive nothing and she would keep everything for herself.

Came the dawn, the two merchants laid formal complaint before the Commissioners for Piracy in Cornwall, the only problem being that Sir John Killigrew himself sat on the bench at Penryn. Enough evidence was found to implicate Hawkins and Kendal but this was rebutted by one Elizabeth Bowden, who kept a small tavern on the waterfront and testified that they had not so much as stepped out the door the whole night. Chavis and De Oryo sped hotfoot to London seeking justice and returned in the company of Sir Richard Grenville and Mr Edmund Tremayne, who had been ordered by the Earl of Bedford (on the queen's instruction) to determine the truth. They concluded that the whole plot had been contrived by Lady Mary Killigrew – they even found the bundles of stolen leather buried in a cask in the gardens at Arwenack. It was also revealed, moreover, that she had sent a messenger by boat to the Governor of nearby St Mawes Castle to inform him that the Spanish merchants proposed to sail that night and to request him not to hinder them. The other castle, of course, was that of Pendennis, where it was shown that Sir John Killigrew had all day harboured the boarding party destined to carry off the merchantman.

Hawkins, who was the ringleader, said he had been sworn to strict secrecy by Lady Killigrew to keep the whole scheme from her husband. Both he and Kendal were hanged at Launceston, but the imprisoned Lady Killigrew escaped the death penalty, it is thought, at the intervention of the queen herself, and (some say, although there is no evidence to the fact) as the result of a massive pay-off by Sir John, whose name had been cleared by Hawkins' testimony.

One can only guess that Hawkins and Kendall, who have no known graves, went to their deaths with the promise that their dependents would be taken care of. By contrast, a mural monument to the piratical pair Sir John and Lady Mary was erected by their son in St Budock's Church, showing them facing each other and kneeling in prayer.

It spelled the bloody end of the West Country's Prayer Book Rebellion, but where are those 3,000 Cornishmen buried?

THE MASSACRE OF CORNWALL'S PEASANTRY

So many people were executed along Cornwall's roads in the early autumn of 1549 for their part in the Prayer Book Rebellion that the execution squads hunting them down ran out of gallows and most of their 6,000 victims were hanged from trees.

It had begun at Easter of that year when the saying of the Mass in Latin was banned across the land and the new Book of English Common Prayer introduced. This hit Cornwall particularly hard, where English, for the most part, was a foreign language. Thousands of Cornishmen, brandishing scythes and billhooks, resolved to march on London to air their grievances. When they got as far as Exeter they besieged the city, hanged the bishop from his own cathedral and set up a road block on the bridge at a place called Fenny Bridges, between Honiton and Ottery St Mary, awaiting the advance of an army sent by the young king to punish them.

It happened long before the car park was built on the high ground at the edge of the Digby housing development outside Exeter but then, as now, the place is called Clyst Heath and it still commands distant views to the south-east of Woodbury Common. This, according to an eyewitness to the murders, was the place chosen by the avenging army's Lord Russell to look back to his bloody handiwork, still unfolding at the foot of the escarpment. There, below the gorse of the open heathland, the village of Clyst St Mary was still burning. It was there that the villagers and the Cornish protesters, more than a thousand souls in that place that afternoon, had already been butchered, their bodies thrown from the bridge and into the stream, while a few remaining diehards chose to suffer a martyr's death, trapped in the houses he had ordered to be put to the torch. Worse was to come. For this was a little before sunset at a quarter to eight in the evening on Monday, 5 August 1549, and here, at the high point of the heath, Russell sat astride his charger, at the head of his army, sent by the boy King Edward VI to punish the 'rebels' of Devon and Cornwall who had refused to adopt his Book of Common Prayer.

But now the victorious army, preparing to camp for the night, saw something to the east that made them put aside their cooking pots and reach once more for their still-bloodied weapons. The last rays of the setting sun had glinted on the spears and helmets of an approaching army. Or so they would have history believe. John Hooker, one of Exeter's defenders and later the man to chronicle the city's account of the siege, wrote:

> Looking back towards Woodbury (they) saw and espied upon Woodbury hill a great company assembled; arching forward, and suspect(ed) that they were a new supply appointed to follow and come upon them. Whereupon it was concluded, that the prisoners (their hands already bound behind their backs) whom they had before taken at the windmill (at Aylesbeare) and in the town, who were a great number, and which if they were newly set upon, might be a detriment and a peril unto them, should be all killed: which forthwith was done, every man making a dispatch of his prisoners.

It took them all of ten minutes to slit the throats of their captives, reports the historian Frances Rose-Troup, who wrote in 1913 in her book *The Western Rebellion, 1549*:

> Ere darkness fell the cries for mercy and the screams of those being murdered rang through the fields and lanes – as each soldier butchered

his victim – nor age or youth were regarded and the shambles thus created made a terrible blot upon the scrutcheon of the Royal forces.

Two thousand more rebels, armed with little more than pitchforks and billhooks, were annihilated on the same ground the following morning, as they left their siege of the city and rallied to join battle with the seasoned professionals of Russell's army, many of whom were German and Italian mercenaries, and walked into the iron wall of Russell's cannons.

So what became of the now 3,000 bodies that lay scattered across Clyst Heath and what memorial is there to their passing? If truth be known, with none left alive to mourn their deaths, they were left there to rot. For in the retribution that followed the lifting of the siege of Exeter, there began a manhunt down through Cornwall that saw 6,000 more 'commons' put to the sword or hanged by the death squads that were now turned loose upon the region. It was said that there was not a tree in Cornwall that did not have a body hanging from it. Rose-Troup writes:

> Three centuries later, in the middle of the 19th century, the virgin soil of the once desolate heath was turned up by the plough, disclosing a vast number of bones, which not only bore witness to the terrible carnage on the spot, but, by the enormous size of many, indicated that the men were of no mean stature [broad-shouldered bowmen?] Here lay all that was mortal of many a brave man who fell fighting desperately in defence of his faith, or was a victim of the cruel massacre of the previous day.

So did the veteran Lord Russell, aged 64 (with just one eye) and the sun already set below the horizon behind him, really spy an approaching army through a pall of black smoke – or had he already made up his mind to rid himself of the great burden of these peasants, none of whom would be worth a penny in ransom? John Hooker, an 'eyewitness' to this event, was in fact still holed up in Exeter. Perhaps, then, this was simply another case of a victor dictating his own version of events for the history books?

Stand at the edge of that shopping centre's car park today, where and when the sun still sets to the west at 7.51 p.m. every 5 August, and look across to Woodbury Common to the east through several miles of twilight and 450 years of history and your guess will be as good as the next man's.

Did the admiral drown or was he murdered?

CLOUDESLEY SHOVELL'S HORRIFIC SHIPWRECK

He had the oddest of names but he was nevertheless a famous naval commander, a precursor of Nelson, an undoubted hero of his or any other age and Britain was so shaken by the circumstances of his tragic death that Queen Anne herself stepped forward and paid for his funeral and entombment in Westminster Abbey. The man was Admiral Sir Cloudesley Shovell and he perished as a consequence of a great storm off the Isles of Scilly in 1707 when four ships of the fleet under his command were smashed to pieces on rocks as they returned from the Mediterranean. There was not a single survivor and the 2,000 men lost in that one dreadful night made it the greatest loss of life ever recorded by the Royal Navy.

At about eight o'clock on the night of 22 October 1707, while returning with the fleet to England after the campaign at Toulon, Shovell's flagship, HMS *Association*, struck rocks near the Isles of Scilly and sank within three to four minutes. All 800 men on board were drowned – including his two stepsons. Three more ships hit rocks nearby: HMS *Eagle*, HMS *Romney* and HMS *Firebrand* were all lost.

Very few people could swim in the eighteenth century and those very few contemporary accounts of sailors swimming more properly describe men flailing their arms or at most attempting a crude dog paddle in an attempt to keep their heads above water. Even fewer, therefore, would have been in any position to offer any assistance to a shipmate at the time of a wreck. Yet remarkably, although he was 57 years of age at his death – apparently by drowning – a family tradition recounted that as a boy in the Second Dutch War, Shovell had carried despatches in his mouth, swimming through enemy fire. The very few who may have been able to scramble ashore that night might have found something equally terrible awaiting them. This is Daniel Defoe, the author of *Robinson Crusoe*, writing about the disaster when he was in the Scillies some few years after the event. It was autumn and he was staying on St Mary when he wrote:

> It had blown something hard in the night, the sands were cover'd with country people running too and fro' to see if the sea had cast up any thing of value. This the seamen call 'going a shoring'; and it seems they do often find good purchase: Sometimes also dead bodies are cast up here, the consequence of shipwrecks among those fatal rocks and islands; as also broken pieces of ships, casks, chests, and almost every thing that will float, or roll on shore by the surges of the sea. Nor is it seldom that the voracious country people scuffle and fight about the right to what they find, and that in a desperate manner, so that this part of Cornwall may truly be said to be inhabited by a fierce and ravenous people; for they are so greedy, and eager for the prey, that they are charg'd with strange, bloody, and cruel dealings, even sometimes with one another; but especially with poor distressed seamen when they come on shore by force of a tempest, and seek help for their lives, and where they find the rocks themselves not more merciless than the people who range about them for their prey.

It was a superstitious belief among seafaring folk in Cornwall that if those who went to sea were taken by the sea then it was God's will – or at the very least that it was fate. That said, to save one's brother from drowning by reaching out your hand or throwing him a line would be 'expected'.

But to save a stranger – a foreigner – to snatch him from his preordained, fateful end was to challenge fate and invite one's own watery demise.

> The cruel and covetous natives of the strand, the wreckers of the seas and rocks for flotsam and jetsam held as an axiom and an injunction to be strictly obeyed.

> Save a stranger from the sea,
> And he will turn your enemy!

No court martial or official enquiry was ever called to determine the exact cause of the disaster but a fascinating on-the-spot report from the scene came two years later. It took the form of a two-page, handwritten document made by a young man, Edmund Herbert, who was later to become Deputy Paymaster General of the Marine Regiments. This was 'lost' until 1883, when it was published by the Society of Antiquaries. It made grim reading for those who had previously been peddled a highly varnished, not to say richly embroidered, version of the truth. Presumably promising them anonymity, Herbert talked to the people who stripped the bodies and 'reaped the harvest of the storm' and made his notes during his residence on St Mary's 'of such particulars as came to his knowledge'. His notes begin with the discovery of Sir Cloudesley's body:

> [He] was found on shore at Porthellick Cove in St Marie's Island, stripped of his shirt, waist coat, by two women, which shirt had his name at ye gusset at his waist; where, by order of Mr — he was buried 4 yards off ye sands; which place I myself view'd & as was by his grave, came by said woman who first saw him after he was stripped. His ring was also lost from off his hand, which however left ye impression on his finger, as also of a second. Sir Cloudesley was the first man came on shore, saving one, of those lost in the wreck and his chest which was by him taken up floating. Many that saw him said his head was the largest that ever they had seen, and not at all swell'd with the waters, neither had he any bruise or fear about him, save only a small scratch above one of his eyes like that of a pin. Was a very lusty, comely man, and very fat.

There came on shore in or very near ye same cove the stern of Sr C.'s barge, which gives ground to believe he had time to get in it with some of his crew, tho' most people are not of that mind; Captain Loads, Sr John and Mr James Narborough [Shovell's stepsons, aged 22 and 23] also the Bishop Trelawney's son, (and Shovell's pet dog) being all cast on shore on St Marie's Island, give further matter of credit. Mr Child, Purser of the Arundel caused him to be taken up (from the shallow, beachside grave) and knew him to be Sir Cloudesley by a certain black mole under his left ear, as also by the first joint of one of his forefingers being broken inwards formerly by playing at Tables; the said joint of his finger was also small and taper, as well as standing somewhat inwards; he had likewise a shot in his right arm, another in his left thigh.

So what led to the disaster? The young Edmund Herbert consulted his note taking with this:

About one or two after noon on the 22nd October Sir C. call'd a council & examined ye Masters which latitude they were in; all agreed to be in that of Ushant on ye coast of France, except Sr W. Jumpers, Master of ye Lenox, who believ'd them to be nearer Scilly, & yet in 3 hours should be up in sight of, which unfortunately happen'd'.

But Sir Cloud listened not to a single person whose opinion was contrary to ye whole fleet. (They then alter'd their opinion and thought themselves to be on ye coast of France, but a lad on board ye [deleted] said the light they made was Scilly light, tho' all the ships crew swore at & gave him ill language for it; howbeit he continu'd in his assertion, and what they made to be a sail and a ship's lanthorn prov'd to be a rock and ye Light aforementioned, which rock ye lad call'd ye Great Smith, of ye truth of which at day-break they was all convinced.

There is still a memorial to be seen at Porthellick Cove where Shovell's body was washed ashore but there is a greater one in Westminster Abbey where his body was finally taken and laid to rest. It had been carried in great state through the West Country – where every town and village turned out to pay its respects. His embalmed body was taken first to his home in Frith Street, Soho, before being finally interred in Westminster Abbey at midnight on 22 December 1707. The heartbroken Lady Elizabeth Shovell offered a reward for the return of the rings that had been stolen from her husband's fingers. Just one of many local fairy stories tells how, thirty years later, an old Scillonian lady made a deathbed confession to a priest that she had found the admiral alive on the beach but hastily despatched him and took his rings. She kept them hidden all her life, the story goes, too frightened to try to find a buyer.

This happy-ever-after version of events tells how they were returned to the good lady, who was overjoyed at their return. Alas the truth is that they were neither found nor returned. Elizabeth herself had died some twenty-five years after her husband, on 15 April 1732, and is buried in St Paulinus Church, Crayford, Kent. Her two sons are buried at Old Church, St Mary's.

Nobody lives forever, but sometimes people try.

A TOMB WITH A VIEW

This is a grisly tale of one Sir James Tillie (1645–1713), described charitably as 'something of a rogue' by one contemporary Cornish chronicler and by another as 'an extraordinary man of dubious character who was honoured by some but loved by none'. The fact that he was also stripped of his heraldic arms by order of the king, the belief that he was also a counterfeiter, a double-dealing lawyer and perhaps even a murderer did nothing to endear him to the good folk of the neighbourhood of the 'castle' he built for himself near St Mellion.

They were distrustful of him during life and fearful of his corpse after death, which, rather than being buried, he had ordered to be placed sitting upright in an armchair, fully clothed, gazing out over his house and estates where he could keep an eye on everything and everybody. For Tillie believed that he would come back to life within two years, to pick up where he had left off. He even named the grassy hill where his open-fronted tower or 'mausoleum' was built, Mount Ararat. A confessed Dissenter as far as his religious beliefs were concerned, his Biblical nomination of his chosen place of temporary rest suggests that he expected to follow in Noah's footsteps by emerging safely from his own ark after the rest of humanity had been swept away.

Tillie was indeed an extraordinary person, so too was his climb to infamy and fortune. He was born the son of a labourer and while living at St Keverne his father managed to get his bright-as-a-button son employed as 'a servant or horseman' to Sir John Coryton, of West Newton Ferrers, 'who afterwards, by his assistance helped him to study Law under an Attorney – in London – so that he could then become his Steward', never guessing that he was already nursing an ambitious, stop-at-nothing viper in his bosom.

William Hals, in his writing of *The History of Cornwall*, says that in his role as Steward and 'by his Care and Industry he soon grew Rich' – probably by helping himself from the till of old, trusting Sir John. So much so that he was able to marry Margaret, one of the five daughters of Sir Henry Vane, a staunch Parliamentarian who lost his head at the Reformation. The marriage lasted just two years before Margaret died suddenly, while Tillie added to his own fortune, estate and social connections. (Hals, something of a gossip as well as an historian, sat on the grand jury of the county court and saw and knew much that was going on behind the scenes in his part of Cornwall.) Tillie's riches 'grew at an even greater pitch' and shortly after James II came to the throne, Hals adds:

> this gentleman by a great sum of money and false representation of himself obtained the favour of knighthood at his hands: but that the King, some short while after being informed that Mr. Tillie was at first but a Groom or Horseman to Sir John Coryton, that he was no Gentleman of Blood or arm, and yet gave for his Coat-armour the arms of Count Tillye of Germany, ordered the Heralds to enquire into this matter.

Alas, Tillie was rumbled and his house in London was entered, by order of the king, whose men 'took down those arms, tore others in pieces, and fastened them all to Horse tails and drew them through the streets, to his perpetual Disgrace and imposed a fine of £200 upon him for so doing'.

Nothing daunted, he picked himself up, brushed himself off and married Elizabeth, the widow of his then new master, Sir John Coryton the Younger. What scandal ensued; Sir John died suddenly, aged just 42 and in great agony – some say by poisoning. Hals continues:

> He very soon after Married the Lady, with whom Common fame said he was too familiar before, so that he became possest of her goods and chattels, and a great Jointure. Whereby he liveth in much pleasure and comfort in this place, admiring himself for the Bulk of his Riches and the Arts and Contrivances by which he got it – some of which were altogether unlawful.

In short, Tillie joined his and what was briefly Elizabeth's estates together, considerably improving his wealth. He had grandiose ideas of himself and not only commissioned a 'castle' to be built but also had a statue of himself made, to stand outside the castle.

He died in 1713. His long-suffering wife Elizabeth survived him but they had no children, though Tillie was anxious to found a dynasty and left a will to ensure that this would come about. He named his nephew, James Woolley, heir providing he changed his name and undertook various conditions, all of which were to be performed by him and his successors forever, in the form of the upkeep and repairs to some ramifications that were to be added to his chosen lookout post, under penalty of losing both lands and rents.

When they were quite sure that the demanding Tillie was dead, Elizabeth and Tillie's servants carried out his final instructions to the letter. He was, within the hour, redressed from top to bottom in his finest clothes, his shoulder-length wig freshly powdered and placed firmly on his head, rings pushed on to his fingers – while the body was still warm – gloves upon his hands, silk stockings fed up his somewhat short and stubby legs and ribbon-laced shoes upon his feet. He was then carefully arranged, sitting bolt upright in his favourite armchair, his wrists wired to the arms. Then, with great ceremony, six men lifted their handiwork and carried it outside to the spot he had chosen for himself – an open-fronted, purpose-built stone platform at the top of a flight of steps – facing out over the favourite view of his great house and estate, where they could see him and he could see them. This was a brick-built 'folly' that took the form of a substantial open-top tower-come-mausoleum overlooking the 'castle' he had built for himself on a greenfield site high above a bend on the River Tamar in Paynters Cross, near to St Mellion. Here, the views were – and are – stunning. Unsurprisingly, he named this heaven-on-earth house after himself, declaring it to be Pentillie Castle.

There the corpse remained unburied, through three winters and almost four long, hot summers, waiting for what he said would be his certain physical resurrection which, he had told them all, would come to pass within two years and he had even ordained that fresh food and drink were to be carried to the spot and placed in front of him at intervals. Alas for him – and Elizabeth too perhaps – his prophecy did not come to pass and, as William Hals reported somewhat graphically as he put down his quill after reporting on the whole sorry episode:

> However, I hear lately, notwithstanding this his promise of returning in two years to Pentillie, that Sir James's body is eaten out with worms, and his bones or skeleton fallen down to the ground from the chair wherein it was seated, about four years after it was set up; his wig, books, wearing apparel, also rotten in the chair where it was first laid.

A roof and then an upper chamber were added later but these collapsed and it was thought that the bones of Sir James were collected by Mary Jemima, the last of the Tillie family and the heiress who carried Pentillie to the Coryton family about 1770, and transferred to the churchyard of St Mellion. But not so. Although Tillie's sense of timing was out by a mile, his physical body was resurrected – most likely by workmen on the estate – and is now at rest beneath the floor of his mausoleum. This only came to light in 2012 when conservation work was being carried out. The skeletal remains of a man were found in a chamber beneath the floor of the current folly and today's owner of Pentillie Castle, Ted Coryton, said, 'There is not really any doubt about who the remains belong to'.

Tilly was a celebrated atheist of his age. He was also, reportedly, something of a wit. Was he therefore a madman to be buried in that way or was he perhaps simply determined to ridicule the whole idea of the resurrection itself? If the latter, it was a pretty poor joke but a joke played in an age that had witnessed a bloody civil war and saw first one king beheaded and then another deposed – all in the name of religion.

So perhaps Sir James Tillie has had the last laugh after all, sitting underneath his tomb all along and still perhaps, waiting for that second coming? But the last word belongs to the Restoration playwright, Thomas Otway: 'Ambition is a lust that is never quenched, but grows more inflamed and madder by enjoyment.' Tillie, the wit, would surely have felt amused but a little cheated by departing this life just one day short of his sixty-eighth birthday.

The Liskeard man chosen by Collingwood to take the news of Trafalgar to England was almost pipped at the post by one of Nelson's own 'band of brothers'.

THE RACE HOME FROM TRAFALGAR

In the long history of our Great South West Road, the most important and certainly the best documented of its stories is of a race undertaken in November 1805 by two serving officers in Nelson's Navy. The first of them, and the hero of our story, was Devon-born Lieutenant John Richards Lapenotière. An eyewitness to the Battle of Trafalgar, south of Cadiz, he carried Collingwood's top-secret dispatches back to England, detailing the battle and telling of the death of Nelson.

Lapenotière was the commander of a dispatch vessel, His Majesty's Schooner *Pickle*, and was ordered to reach the nearest English port, 'saving neither spar nor canvas' to take the news to the Admiralty in London. Tradition dictated that any man charged with such a mission would receive a 500-guinea purse, a 100-guinea presentation sword and – most importantly for a 35-year-old widower supporting his two small daughters and a widowed father on his £85-a-year lieutenant's pay – a promotion. He set off at 11.30 in the morning on Sunday, 27 October, a full week after the battle but the first time that there had been a lull in the great storm that had followed it.

The other man was Captain John Sykes of the sloop HMS *Nautilus*, patrolling near Cape St Vincent off the coast of southern Portugal. One of Nelson's inner circle of captains, Sykes had been on station since the end of August and knew nothing of the battle or Nelson's death when he intercepted the homeward bound *Pickle* and ordered her to heave-to. After an hour on board *Pickle*, Sykes let Lapenotière go on his way before heading to Lisbon, a neutral port, to report to the British Ambassador there so that the news could be spread throughout war-torn Europe. Sykes handed a hastily written note to the occupants of a pilot gig he hailed at the mouth of Lisbon's River Tagus. This accomplished – or so he thought – he set sail again, hard on the heels of *Pickle*, making for the little ship's home port, Plymouth, where he assumed Lapenotière to be headed. The note was never received and may have been passed to an American warship then at anchor in Lisbon Harbour. It would certainly explain why news of Trafalgar was printed in a handbill in Maine and then a newspaper in New York before the official *London Gazette* reached America in early December.

But *Pickle* had run into trouble. She had encountered a great storm in the Bay of Biscay and was swamped by an enormous sea. Only by jettisoning her eight cannon and by manning the pumps for two days and nights did she weather the calamity. After the storm came flat calm when the exhausted crew was forced to take to the sweeps (oars) to keep the ship crawling towards the shoreline. Lapenotière finally made landfall at Falmouth at 11.30 in the morning of Monday, 4 November 1805. From here he immediately took the first of a series of rented post-chaises – the fastest things on four wheels in Georgian England – to speed him on his way to London.

Post-chaises were rented out by the larger inns along the highway, where the horses were changed every 15 miles or so, along with the drivers, or rather riders, for these 'postillions' – men who knew their own particular stretch of road like the backs of their hands – were not coachmen but jockeys, who rode one of the front pair of horses. Although it had not rained in England since 30 October, the roads out of Cornwall were bad and deeply rutted but Lapenotière was duty bound to keep moving. The Cornwall part of the journey took him from Falmouth, first to Truro, then on to Fraddon, where he changed horses at the Blue Anchor, thence across the moors to Bodmin, Launceston and Okehampton, Crockernwell and Exeter.

Food was snatched in stable yards during the time that it took to change horses or carriages. He slept as best he could in the corner of the bucking, rocking coach, wrapped in his boat cloak, keeping his legs warm in the dry, knee-deep straw that was pushed in through the doorway before it was slammed shut. His small sea chest, propped beside him on the forward-facing bench seat, contained his best uniform, a change of linen, soap and razor and, most importantly, a purse of money issued to all dispatch vessels to allow messengers like him to pay their way at the coaching inns that rented out these flying carriages. He made the epic 271-mile dash in a little over thirty-six hours, stopping twenty-one times to change horses and postillions. Where the road was especially bad or the hills steep, he rented four horses, as his receipts show. His post chaise from Crockernwell to Exeter, for example, cost the Admiralty £1 16s; from Exeter to Honiton £1 17s; but from Honiton to Axminster, where there are still steep gradients, he had four horses hitched and paid £2 14s. And so on. Expenses claimed for the entire journey, later reimbursed by an Admiralty clerk, totalled £46 19s 1d – a tidy sum and more than half a lieutenant's pay in 1805. (Lapenotière had to write to the Admiralty twice after making his claim and didn't actually receive the money until the following spring.)

Although he had no way of knowing it, from Honiton onwards Lapenotière's journey became a race – for Sykes, aboard the *Nautilus*, landing at Portsmouth a few hours after *Pickle* had dropped anchor off Falmouth and finding no news of *Pickle* had also set out for London without delay. The race was on, each man unaware of the location – or the existence – of the other and both carriages, perhaps, leap-frogging each other in the darkness as first one stopped to change horses at a particular inn, and then the other. By the time they reached London, Lapenotière was barely an hour ahead, where he found the city wrapped in the thickest fog in living memory. He finally reached the Admiralty at one o'clock in the morning of Wednesday, 6 November. Lapenotière came down Whitehall from what would one day become Trafalgar

Square, while Sykes's post-chaise had taken the route along the Chelsea embankment, arriving just a few minutes later. The 1,300-mile dash by sea and land was over. Lapenotière had won and the two men shook hands in front of the empty fireplace in the great echoing entrance hall of the Admiralty.

Messengers were immediately sent to Windsor to break the news to the king, and Lapenotière, freshly shaved and changed into his best blues, was sent close on their heels through the darkness of the early morning to give his first-hand account of what he had witnessed. It is almost certain that in the presence of Queen Charlotte and the royal princesses, he used the cutlery on King George III's breakfast table to set out the disposition of the fleets: forks for the French, spoons for the Spanish and knives for the British. This is perhaps borne out by the fact that as he left Windsor the king presented Lapenotière with a silver muffineer, or sugar shaker, that the young officer had employed to represent the *Victory*.

Later that same day, the young lieutenant must have been exhausted when he was promoted commander by their Lordships in the Admiralty itself. The Patriotic Fund gave him a sword worth 100 guineas, which stayed in the family for over a hundred years. So too did the silver muffineer – now part of the civic treasure of Liskeard, where he lived at that time. His sword and his portrait are in the National Maritime Museum at Greenwich. He also received 500 guineas prize money, which enabled him to marry before Christmas of that same year to his second wife, Mary Ann, with whom he had seven more children.

Lapenotière obtained post-rank to captain on 1 August 1811 and after a distinguished career retired to live quietly at Roseland, outside the village of Menheniot, Cornwall, where he became a church warden. We know from the minutes of a church meeting that he opposed the idea of having a chiming clock installed in the tower – which 'would be enough to waken the dead', or so he reckoned. Alas, he was unsuccessful in his objection. He died in 1834, aged 63, and at his particular request was buried 'on the quiet side of the church', away from the clock face and its chiming bell, so that he 'might sleep undisturbed through Eternity' – a simple enough request from a career officer in Nelson's Navy, a man who had seen enough action to last any man several lifetimes.

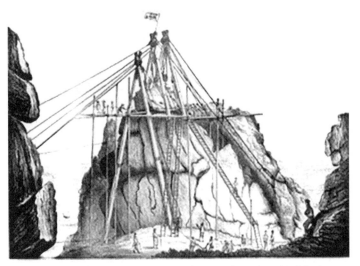

The single act of folly that dogged a man throughout his life.

THE LIEUTENANT AND THE TOPPLING
OF THE LOGAN STONE

The Vandals wore themselves out a hundred years or so after sacking Rome but it was sufficient time to introduce the word vandalism to the language and the act itself to a wider world. In nineteenth-century Cornwall, for instance, it manifested itself again when one Lieutenant Goldsmith, a man who has been described separately by contemporary writers as 'bored' and 'silly', the commanding officer of a Royal Navy revenue cutter, encouraged his crew to manhandle an ancient, 80-ton granite logan, or 'rocking boulder', into the sea. The logan had been set by nature within an Iron Age fort at the end of a rocky promontory near the village of Treen in the far west of Cornwall and was renowned for curing childhood diseases. A sick child could be made well again by being taken to the stone at certain times of the year and rocked. The charm was broken, said the Cornish, and thousands of years of magic were dislodged when Goldsmith toppled the rock.

The *Gentleman's Magazine* reported:

On April 8, 1824, a party of sailors belonging to H.M. cutter Nimble, commanded by Lieutenant Hugh Goldsmith, R. N. (the 34-year-old relative of the poet Oliver Goldsmith), came on shore for the purpose of removing from its situation that great curiosity the Logging (rocking) Stone. This act of vandalism has excited the greatest indignation at Penzance, as it will in every part of Cornwall, and throughout the kingdom. It appears that Lieutenant Goldsmith landed at the head of fourteen of his men, and with the assistance of handspikes and a hand-screw, called by the sailors jack-in-the-box, with much labour and perseverance threw over the stone. What renders the act most atrocious is, that two poor families, who derived a subsistence from attending visitors to the stone, are now deprived of the means of support. The Logan Stone, thus displaced, would have rolled down from the tor on which it had rested and have shot into the sea, had it not happily been arrested by a cleft in the rock.

Cornwall was inflamed and Goldsmith received death threats from local fishermen should he next make landfall in the county. A gathering of magistrates was called to demand of the Admiralty what their intentions might be 'against the perpetrator of this wanton act of mischief'. Their Lordships responded by demanding that he replace the block as found, at his own expense, or forfeit his commission. As the expense would be wholly beyond his means, a Mr Davies Gilbert, a very kindly old gentleman:

ever ready to render assistance to any one in trouble, readily assisted, and having travelled into Cornwall and seen the damage done, applied to the Admiralty for the loan of the proper apparatus, capstan, blocks and chains to be furnished by the dockyard at Devonport. This agreed he very liberally subscribed £150 towards the project.

What Goldsmith had to say on this whole sorry state of affairs is recorded in a letter he wrote to his mother on 24 April 1824 in a blatant attempt to try to square things away with the poor distraught woman:

The facts in question, my dear mother, are these: On the 8th of this month we were off the Land's End, near the spot where the Rock stood. Our boats were creeping along shore beneath it for some goods which, we suspected, might be sunk in the sands near it. I took the opportunity of landing to look at the Logan Rock with my Mate; and hearing that it was not in the power of men to remove it, I took it into my head to try my skill, and, at this time (half-past four o'clock p.m.), the boats having finished what they had to do, and it blowing too fresh for them to creep any longer, I took them and their crew with me, and, having landed at the foot of the rocks, we all scrambled up the precipice. We had with us, at first, three handspikes, with which we tried to move the Rock, but could not do it.

By 'move the rock' of course he really meant – displace it. A child could move it on its pivot:

The handspikes were then laid aside, and the nine men who were with me took hold of the Rock by the edge, and with great difficulty set it in a rocking motion, which became so great, that I was fearful of bidding them try to stop it lest it should fall back upon us, and away it went unfortunately, clean over upon its side, where it now rests. There was not an instrument of any kind or description near the Rock when thrown over, except one handspike, and that I held in my hand, but which was of no use in upsetting the Rock; and this is the truth, and nothing but the truth, as I hope for salvation.

For my part, I had no intention, or the most distant thought, of doing mischief, even had I thrown the Rock into the sea. I was innocently, as my God knows, employed, as far as any bad design about me. I knew not that the Rock was so idolized in this neighbourhood, and you may imagine my astonishment when I found all Penzance in an uproar. I was to be transported at least; the newspapers have traduced me, and made me worse than a murderer, and the base falsehoods in them are more than wicked. But here I am, my dear mother, still holding up my head, boldly conscious of having only committed an act of inadvertency. Be not uneasy – my character is yet safe; and you have nothing on that score to make you uneasy. I have many friends in Penzance: among them the persons most interested in the Rock, and many who were most violent now see the thing in its true light. I intend putting the bauble in its place again, and hope to get as much credit as I have anger for throwing it down.

The Victorian writer and social historian, the Reverend Sabine Baring-Gould, later wrote somewhat succinctly:

> The letter is disingenuous, and is the composition of a man impudent and conceited. He knew the estimation in which the Logan Rock was held, and it was because William Borlase (the Cornish antiquary, geologist and naturalist) had pronounced it impossible of displacement that he resolved to displace it. He pretends that he tried to 'move' it, whereas from the context it is clear that he intended to throw it down, and for this purpose had brought the handspikes.

Encouraged no doubt by the Admiralty to redress the balance in favour of the Senior Service – which understandably was at rock bottom with the Cornish at this time – *The Royal Cornwall Gazette* put more than a modicum of spin on its reporting of the events that transpired on 2 November:

> Endeavour to conceive a group of rocks of the most grand and romantic appearance, forming an amphitheatre, with multitudes seated on the irregular masses, or clinging to its precipices: conceive a huge platform carried across an abyss from rock to rock, and upon it three capstans manned by British seamen. Imagine the lofty masts which are seen rearing their heads, from which ropes are connected with chains in many a fold and of massive strength. A flag waves over all: the huge stone is in the midst. Every eye is directed to the monstrous bulk. Will it break its chains? Will it fall and spread ruin? Or will it defy the power that attempts to stir it? Will all the skill and energy, and strength and hardihood, have been exerted in vain? We shall soon know: expectation sits breathless; and at last it moves. All's well! Such was the first half-hour. In two hours it was suspended in the air, and vibrated; but art was triumphant, and held the huge leviathan fast.
>
> I will not detail the labour of two successive days; but come to the last moment. At twenty minutes past four on Tuesday afternoon a signal was given that the rock was in its place and that it logged

again. This was announced by a spectator. But where was Lieutenant Goldsmith? Why does not he announce it? He has called his men around him: his own and their hats are off: he is addressing them first, and calling upon them to return thanks to God, through whose aid alone the work had been done —a work of great peril and hazard — and by His blessing without loss of life or limb.

After this appropriate and solemn act, he called upon them to join in the British sailors' testimony of joy, three cheers; and then turned with all his gallant men to receive the re-echoing cheers of the assembled multitude. That Lieutenant Goldsmith, whose character — like the rock — is replaced on a firm basis, may have an opportunity of exerting his great talents and brave spirit in the service of his profession, is the sincere wish of all this neighbourhood. In the presence of vast crowds, ladies waving their handkerchiefs, and men firing feux de joie, the block was raised, Mr. Goldsmith, his natural conceit overcoming his sense of vexation, superintending the operation. But, although replaced, it was no longer so perfectly balanced as before. As one wrote who was present at the time, 'it rocked differently, though well enough to satisfy the people'.

A small group of Cornish folk, doubtless carried away in the spirit of the moment, actually proposed after the re-erection of the stone to give to Lieutenant Goldsmith a dinner and a silver cup. But this did not come to pass. Subsequently the *Western Antiquary reported*: 'The result of this foolhardy act was that Lieutenant Goldsmith was pecuniarily ruined, whilst the natives of the locality reaped a rich harvest by pointing out the fallen stone to visitors.'

Goldsmith moved on, returned to service and died at sea off Saint Thomas, in the West Indies, on passage from Barbados to Jamaica. It was 8 October 1841, where, still a lieutenant aged 51, he had been the commanding officer of HM steam vessel *Megaera*.

In the same way that Coleridge's Ancient Mariner's destiny was shaped by his encounter with an albatross, so with Goldsmith's ill-fated Cornish escapade. Of his forty-one-word obituary in the *Gentleman's Magazine*, the last twenty-one of them are used to remind anyone who might have forgotten: 'It was he who removed, and afterwards succeeded in replacing, the celebrated Druidical monument, the Logan Stone, near the Land's End.'

It took something to make Nelson's Navy blush.

DOLLY'S ANCIENT TONGUE

It was said of Dolly Pentreath in her native village of Mousehole that, 'She had a mouth on her!' But in defence of the lady it should perhaps be added that her expletives were confined to the Cornish language and she, by many accounts was, historically, the last speaker of that ancient tongue.

Dorothy 'Dolly' Pentreath was baptised on 16 May 1692 and died on 26 December 1777, aged 102. She was one of six children and from the age of 12 earned her living by hawking the fish her father caught, 'selling them in Penzance in the Cornish language, which the inhabitants in general, even the gentry, did then well understand'. This was 1704. When she was in her mid-80s it was written of her that:

> She does, indeed, talk Cornish as readily as others do English, being bred up from a child to know no other language; nor could she (if we may believe her) talk a word of English before she was past twenty years of age. She is poor, and maintained partly by the parish, and partly by fortune-telling and gabbling Cornish.

Many thought her a witch. She never married – although she bore a son who, alas, died in infancy – and although her language was colourful, she had a good heart and a quick wit, as the following story about her in her younger days reveals. This from the pen of J. Henry Harris in *Cornish Saints and Sinners*:

> On one occasion a deserter from a man-of-war fled to her house for refuge, and as there was a cavity in her chimney large enough to contain a man, she thrust him into it, and threw a bundle of dry furze on the fire, and filled the crock with water. Into the middle of the kitchen she drew a 'keeve', (a wooden tub) which she used for washing, and when the naval officer and his men in pursuit burst into her house, Dolly was sitting on a stool, her legs bare and her feet ready to be immersed in the keeve. She screamed out on their entry that she was about to wash her feet, and only waiting for the water to get hot enough. The officer persisted in searching, and she gave tongue in strong and forcible Cornish. She rushed to the door and screamed to the good people of Mousehole. The officer and his men withdrew without having seen and secured their man; and that night a fishing lugger stole out of Mousehole with the deserter on board and made for Guernsey, which in those days was a sort of dumping-ground for all kinds of rascals who were 'wanted' at home.

An earlier historian, one Daines Barrington, was combing Cornwall in 1768 in search of anyone still speaking the old language and was guided to Mousehole by a publican from Penzance. He told him about Dolly but warned him against crossing her – which advice he ignored – and brought her legendary wrath down upon himself. He described her as:

> short of stature, and bends very much with old age, being in her eighty-seventh year, so lusty, however, as to walk hither to Castle Horneck, about three miles, in bad weather, in the morning and back again. She is somewhat deaf, but her intellect seemingly not impaired; has a good memory. When we reached Mousehole I desired to be introduced to her as a person who had laid a wager that there was not one who could converse in Cornish; upon which Dolly Pentreath

spoke in an angry tone for two or three minutes, and in a language which sounded very like Welsh. The hut in which she lived was in a very narrow lane, opposite to two rather better houses, at the doors of which two other women stood, who were advanced in years, and who I observed were laughing at what Dolly said to me. Upon this I asked them whether she had not been abusing me; to which they answered, 'Very heartily', and because I had supposed she could not speak Cornish. I then said that they must be able to talk the language; to which they answered that they could not speak it readily, but that they understood it, being only ten or twelve years younger than Dolly Pentreath.

In the last years of her life, she became a local celebrity for her knowledge of Cornish and was painted by John Opie (1761–1807), and in 1781 a published engraving of her was made by Robert Scaddan. Dolly Pentreath was buried in the churchyard of St Paul Aurelian, where in 1860 a monument in her honour was set up by Louis Lucien Bonaparte, a nephew of Napoleon, and by the vicar of Paul of the time. At the base of her epitaph today is written:

> Honour thy father and thy mother, that thy days may be long in the land which the Lord thy God giveth thee. Exodus xx. 12.

Beneath which, but this time in her native Cornish, is inscribed:

> Gwra pethi de taz ha de mam: mal de Dythiow bethenz hyr war an tyr neb an arleth de dew ryes dees. Exodus xx. 12.

The Cornish chough he found 'inedible' and the country people 'boors'.

DEFOE AS TRAVEL WRITER IN CORNWALL

After writing *Robinson Crusoe*, Daniel Defoe (1660–1731), writer, journalist, pamphleteer and secret agent, packed up his pens, ink and notebooks and found his way down into Cornwall. He was a prolific writer on topics as diverse as politics, crime, religion, marriage, psychology and the supernatural, but in taking what was supposedly this his first ever journey to the far South West, he was ostensibly collecting material for his next book during his 'grand tour' of England.

In fact he had, somehow or other, landed on the shores of Cornwall in unexplained circumstances and witnessed a brief but ferocious naval engagement from a high point near the Lizard Peninsula, 'Upon a former accidental journey into this part of the country during the war with France …' His brief reference to that 'accidental visit' underlines the enigma of a man, much of whose life was cloaked in secrecy.

But here he is, in 1723, crossing the Tamar and doing what he was famed for, spinning yarns:

From Plymouth we pass the Tamar over a ferry to Saltash – a little, poor, shattered town, the first we set foot on in the county of Cornwall. The Tamar here is very wide, and the ferry-boats bad; so that I thought myself well escaped when I got safe on shore in Cornwall.

Saltash seems to be the ruins of a larger place; and we saw many houses, as it were, falling down, and I doubt not but the mice and rats have abandoned many more, as they say they will when they are likely to fall.

There is a strange story of a dog in this town, of whom it was observed that if they gave him any large bone or piece of meat, he immediately went out of doors with it, and after having disappeared for some time would return again; upon which, after some time, they watched him, when, to their great surprise, they found that the poor charitable creature carried what he so got to an old decrepit mastiff, which lay in a nest that he had made among the brakes a little way out of the town, and was blind, so that he could not help himself; and there this creature fed him. On Sundays or holidays, when he found they made good cheer in the house where he lived, he would go out and bring this old blind dog to the door, and feed him there till he had enough, and then go with him back to his habitation in the country again, and see him safe in.

Between Saltash and Liskeard, he remarked:

are many pleasant seats of the Cornish gentry, who are indeed very numerous … they are the most sociable, generous, and to one another the kindest, neighbours that are to be found; and as they generally live, as we may say, together (for they are almost always at one another's houses), so they generally intermarry among themselves, the gentlemen seldom going out of the county for a wife, or the ladies for a husband; from whence they say that proverb upon them was raised, viz., 'That all the Cornish gentlemen are cousins.'

Like so many visitors since, he was drawn to visit the Boscawen Circle, then a somewhat mysterious stone circle:

between Penzance and St Burien, where stands a circle of great stones, not unlike those at Stonehenge, with one bigger than the rest in the middle. They stand about twelve feet asunder, but have no inscription; neither does tradition offer to leave any part of their history upon record, as whether it was a trophy or a monument of burial, or an altar for worship, or what else; so that all that can be learned of them is that here they are.

Shortly after he left, the circle was visited by William Stukeley, an English antiquarian and archaeologist who subsequently enlightened Defoe and the rest of Britain when he wrote that it was the work of the Druids who were part of 'an oriental colony' of Phoenicians who had settled in Britain between the end of Noah's flood and the time of Abraham. The leader of the Phoenician Druids, he said, had been Hercules, who had landed in western Britain and created the Boscawen Circle.

Inevitably, Defoe found his way to Tintagel:

a mark of great antiquity, and every writer has mentioned it; but as antiquity is not my work, I leave the ruins to those that search into antiquity; little or nothing, that I could hear, is to be seen at it; and as for the story of King Arthur being both born and killed there, 'tis a piece of tradition, only on oral history, and not any authority to be produced for it.

Which neatly put the whole subject to bed forever:

We have nothing more of note in this county, that I could see, or hear of, but a set of monumental stones, found standing not far from Bodmyn, called The Hurlers, of which the country, nor all the writers of the country, can give us no good account; so I must leave them as I found them. The game called the Hurlers, is a thing the Cornish men value themselves much upon; I confess, I see nothing in it, but that it is a rude violent play among the boors, or country people; brutish and furious, and a sort of an evidence, that they were, once, a kind of barbarians: It seems, to me, something to resemble the old way of play, as it was then called, with whirle-bats, with which Hercules slew the gyant, when he undertook to clean the Augean stable.

The wrestling in Cornwall, is, indeed, a much more manly and generous exercise, and that closure, which they call the Cornish Hug, has made them eminent in the wrestling rings all over England, as the Norfolk, and Suffolk men, are for their dexterity at the hand and foot, and throwing up the heels of their adversary, without taking hold of him.

But Defoe could not return to London to write up his latest 'letter' of his travels before making mention of Cornwall's famous bird, the chough. Historically, the south-west of the UK, especially Cornwall, was then a stronghold for choughs but after a long decline because of habitat loss and persecution, the last chough disappeared from Cornwall in 1973. Now, thankfully they are making a comeback and the RSPB has said that their return is a milestone in terms of UK range recovery for this 'captivating crow'.

In 1723 Defoe knew that some local people thought the bird to be a reincarnation of King Arthur himself but his report on the subject demonstrates how there were others, like himself, who held no romantic ideas on the subject:

> We saw great numbers of that famous kind of crows, which is known by the name of the Cornish cough, or chough, so the country people call them: the body is black, the legs, feet, and bill of a deep yellow, almost to a red; I could not find that it was affected for any good quality it had, nor is the flesh good to eat, for it feeds much on fish and carrion; it is counted little better than a kite, for it is of ravenous quality, and is very mischievous; it will steal and carry away any thing it finds about the house, that is not too heavy, tho' not fit for its food; as knives, forks, spoons and linen cloths, or whatever it can fly away with, sometimes they say it has stolen bits of firebrands, or lighted candles, and lodged them in the stacks of corn, and the thatch of barns and houses, and set them on fire; but this I only had by oral tradition.

Apart from the earlier mention of *Robinson Crusoe*, Defoe is also renowned for writing *The Fortunes and Misfortunes of the Famous Moll*

Flanders, but one of his lesser-known works, published in 1719, a full four years before his first 'official' visit to Cornwall, is actually set in the Duchy and is believed by many to be based on a real person. The village in which the action takes place was and remains a real place. The book is called called *Dickory Cronke* and it is about a man born in Talskiddy. Talskiddy is a small rural village about 2 miles north of St Columb Major, which is probably one of the smallest villages in Cornwall and is one of only a few villages in Cornwall that has a village green. It also has a duck pond, known by the residents as 'the harbour'. The full title of the book is *Dickory Cronke: The Dumb Philosopher: or, Great Britain's Wonder*. In the preface, Defoe writes that the book contains:

A faithful and very surprising Account how Dickory Cronke, a Tinner's son, in the County of Cornwall, was born Dumb, and continued so for Fifty-eight years; and how, some days before he died, he came to his Speech; with Memoirs of his Life, and the Manner of his Death.

Is the book simply some kind of political rant and entirely fictitious, or is it based on someone he either knew or had heard of? His best known novel, *Robinson Crusoe*, is based in part on the story of the Scottish castaway Alexander Selkirk, who spent four years stranded in the Juan Fernández Islands. Is Dickory Cronke of Talskiddy evidence of that earlier, 'unexpected' journey into Cornwall by Defoe: perhaps when he was, for a time, a secret agent working for the government under the Cornish nobleman Sidney Godolphin? Whichever, the 300-year-old conundrum remains.

A child prodigy, an untaught genius, who within three months of being launched in London was painting portraits for the King.

THEY CALLED HIM 'THE CORNISH WONDER'

In fashionable London in the 1780s Sir Joshua Reynolds, founder and first president of the Royal Academy, called John Opie, 'A wondrous Cornishman, who is carrying all before him. He is Caravaggio and Velasquez in one!'

Back home in humble Trevellas, where he had been born on 16 May 1761, Opie's proud mother would have got the gist of the sentiment but politely pointed out to Sir Joshua that the family called him Jan and his surname was pronounced Oppy – for that was and is the Cornish way. The youngest of five children, Opie was born in Harmony Cottage, Trevellas, which is halfway between St Agnes and Perranporth. His father was a carpenter and his son – like it or not – was apprenticed to him. His mother, Mary Tonkin, who was 48 when her son was born, adored him.

He painted historic subjects and portraits of many great men and women of his day, including members of the British royal family, and earned the nickname 'The Cornish Wonder' because he had been entirely self-taught. Though he rose to become a Royal Academician when only 27, some of his paintings have a gloom about them that may have been coloured by memories of the bleak moors and slag heaps surrounding his childhood home: this and the fact that his upbringing was in a fairly 'puritanical' household.

One life-changing Sunday when he was 11, he was left in the cottage with his father while his mother went to the meeting house. As his father dozed by the fire John seized the opportunity to paint his portrait, something entirely forbidden as 'Sabbath-breaking'. To make matters worse, he woke him from his nap in order to 'get his eyes lightened up'. The likeness was so good, however, that the portrait was shown around the neighbourhood and the walls of the cottage were soon decorated with portraits of most of his relations and playmates. But with a living to earn, painting had to come second – which meant he sometimes got up to paint at three in the morning before his father stirred. He was always easily depressed and once told how he had walked to Redruth, with 2s 6d in his pocket, to buy some colours. Instead he came across a fair and he and his money were soon parted. Trudging back home through wind and rain, he was so overcome with the miserable plight he had brought upon himself that he thought to somehow or other take his own life: as he explained to his mother on his return, 'I love painting more than bread and meat'.

When he was in his early teens, he was working with his father in a grand house at Mithian that had a painting of a farmstead hanging on a wall. When he began to slip off from his allotted work each day to memorise it so that he could paint it for himself at home, his father took him to task. Overhearing the conversation, the owner gave John the loan of the painting until his own version was completed. The finished work was sold to a Mrs Walker, whose son was vicar of St Winnow, for 5 shillings. Young Opie was so astonished that he ran about the house shouting: 'I'm set up for life!' At this, his father is said to have observed, 'That boy'll come to hanging, as sure as a gun.' His sister, Betty, remembered another occasion a few years later when he came home with 30 guineas in his pocket after painting portraits of some of the Prideaux family at Place House, the Elizabethan manor house above Padstow. He threw the coins on the floor and rolled over and over on them in the new coat he had bought for himself shouting, 'See! see! I'm walving [wallowing] in gold!' He then stood and gave his money to their mother.

Opie's artistic abilities eventually came to the attention of local physician and satirist Dr John Wolcot who, in 1775, came to see him at the sawmill where he was working. Recognising a great talent, he bought him out of his apprenticeship and became Opie's mentor; taking him under his wing first at his home in Truro and then on to London, to find fame and fortune with many commissions for work. With Wolcot as his well-connected manager, Opie soon became the talk of the town and just three months after his arrival he was able to pen this letter to his mother and family back in Cornwall. Written from his lodging 'At Mr. Riccard's, Orange Court, Leicester Fields, London, Monday, March 11, 1782', he reported:

Dear Mother, I received my brother's two last letters, and am exceedingly sorry to hear that my father is so poorly; don't let him work any more, I hope he will be better before this arrives. I have all the prospect of success that is possible, having much more business than I can possibly do. I have been with the King and Queen, who were highly pleased with my work, and took two of my pictures, and they are hung up in the King's collection at the Queen's palace. As to my stay here, it will depend on circumstances, as the continuation of employ and the encouragement I may meet with. Many have been in town, years, and have had nothing to do, whilst I, who have been here but two or three months, am known and talked of by everybody. To be known, is the great thing in London. A man may do ever so well, if nobody knows it, it will signify nothing; and among so many thousand and ten thousand people, it is no easy matter to get known. It is cold and very dirty [here], and so full of smoak [*sic*] and fog that you can hardly see the length of your nose, and I should not be able to stir anywhere out by day. If I have time and money I shall certainly come down in the summer.

But the summer of that same year saw him exhibit at the Royal Academy and in the December, and on 20 May 1795 he was married to 'a giddy young socialite, a black-eyed beauty' called Mary Bunn, a City solicitor's daughter. But the match was not a happy one. Mary was used to the company of a wide circle of well-to-do friends and John, although benefitting from the portraits the introductions brought, was very much an inward-looking person. They had married at St Martin-in-the-Fields Church on 4 December 1782 but by 20 May 1795 Mary had had enough and ran off with an army major. The Opies' marriage was dissolved by Act of Parliament in 1796. Opie managed to remain more or less philosophical about it. Walking past St Martin's with a friend who had recently become a devout atheist, the friend remarked, 'Ah! I was christened at that church.' To which Opie replied, 'And I was married in it; they make unsure work there, for it neither holds in wedlock nor in baptism.'

At length the crowds of sitters and callers began to dwindle away, and although this change in fortune hit his pocket hard, it gave Opie the opportunity to produce fewer portraits but more historical compositions, which he had long wanted to do. In 1791 Opie had moved to the house in which he lived for the last sixteen years of his life, in Berners Street, off Oxford Street, and here he passed the happiest days of what was to be his short life. In 1798 he met a young woman at a party and fell instantly in love. Her name was Amelia Alderson, the only child of a Norwich physician: she was 29 and he 37. She was much courted in the fashionable circles of London for her literary and conversational talents, numbered Sir Walter Scott and Wordsworth among her friends and wrote short stories and small novels. They married in London but by mutual agreement chose 8 May for the ceremony, 'Flora Day' in his native Cornwall. Opie was devoted to her and they were most happy in each other's company. He kept an unfinished portrait of his wife in his studio, constantly working on it in order to bring it to the perfection of the sitter.

In 1805 he was appointed a Professor at the Royal Academy and gave a series of lectures that were published after his death, with an introduction written by Amelia. Opie died in April 1807, aged 46, at their home in Berners Street, 'from abdominal paralysis – probably caused by the absorption into his system of lead-vapours from his paints'. He had been due to be knighted later that same year. He was buried in the crypt in St Paul's Cathedral, next to Sir Joshua Reynolds, as he had wished. Several of the Cornish aristocracy were among his pall-bearers, including Sir John St Aubyn, who said of him that 'he did not so much paint to live, as live to paint'. He had painted 508 portraits in all, mostly in oil, and 252 other pictures.

Amelia became a Quaker in 1825 and died some forty-seven years after John's death, on 2 December 1853, aged 84. She was buried in the same grave with her father, in the Friends' burial ground in Norwich. The Opies' long-time plan to visit Cornwall together never came about and it was not until late in the year of 1832 that she finally took the series of long stagecoach journeys to the far west to see the house where he had been born and spend time with her husband's relatives. 'I am here,' she wrote on 26 November 1832, 'with my poor husband's nephew, and his wife and family, which consists of Edward Opie the painter; a boy of ten; and of a gentle and pleasing young woman, named Amelia, after me, at the desire of my poor sister (this was John's sister Betty, who had also passed on). The whole family have soft pleasing manners; in short, I like them all.'

Her last day in Trevellas ended where this account of John Opie's life began:

> Yesterday I dined at Harmony Cottage, where my husband and all the family were born and bred. It is a most sequestered [hidden away] cottage, whitewashed and thatched; a hill rising high above it, and another in front; trees and flower-beds before it, which in summer must make it a pretty spot. Now, it is not a tempting abode; but there are two good rooms, and I am glad to have seen it.

It's a 300-mile car journey from Newlyn to London today but on foot in 1851 it was 350 miles of mud or dust.

THE QUEEN AND THE CORNISH FISHWIFE

Not too many Cornish fishwives visited the Great Exhibition of 1851 in London's Hyde Park and only one, so far as is known, walked there, in her eighty-forth year, met Queen Victoria and travelled back to Penzance in some style.

Her name was Mary Kelynack and she was born at Tolcarne, in Madron, in the parish of Penzance on Christmas Day, 1766. She was part of a long line of Kelynacks, all of whom had been fisherfolk and seamen at Newlyn and its neighbourhood. Many of them it seems, had some remarkable qualities and Mary was no exception.

More than a generation before, a Philip Kelynack, a physically powerful man, faced down a mob that was attempting to manhandle John Wesley, the Methodist preacher, on his first trip to Newlyn, preaching against the sinfulness of wrecking and smuggling. But in the late summer of 1851 we find Mary Kelynack at home in the Fragdon area of the seaside village of Newlyn, desperately hard up. Though entitled to a small state pension, she had been struggling unsuccessfully to wring it out of the local authorities: at which point she decided to put the matter before the Lord Mayor of London, whom she believed to be supreme in such matters. She bided her time and carefully planned her visit to coincide with the Great Exhibition. This ran from 1 May through to 15 October 1851 and admission prices, she knew, became cheaper as the year wore on.

The price for an opening day ticket was 3 guineas (more than £300 in today's money), then reducing to 5s per day until 22 May. Certain days were then priced at 1s (£5 or so today). These 'Shilling Days', as they became known, were designed to attract 'the industrial classes' – a class that did not include impoverished Cornish fishwives. But Mary saved and set out halfway through September to see for herself the great wonder of the age, the Crystal Palace in London.

She carried a wicker basket on her back, the so-called 'cowal' used by Cornish fisherwomen to carry the catch. The weight of the cowal was borne by wide webbing straps and carried much like a rucksack, keeping both hands free to either gut fish and throw it over her shoulder or, in this instance, to wield a heavy walking staff or stick to help her along the way. Around her shoulders and tucked in at the waist of her dress she wore a shawl. Her 'Sunday best' shawl had a paisley pattern, brought south from Scotland by fishermen and worn by many of the women of Newlyn in those times. This was neatly folded and carried in the cowal along with her other few personal belongings.

Her walk from Newlyn to the outskirts of London took five weeks. Where she slept or how she sustained herself along the way is not known but it is known that she found a very humble lodging for herself above a shop in Homer Place, off Crawford Street, in Marylebone, at that time one of the poorest quarters of London. Her epic journey and her story must have preceded her, indeed it had probably been a talking point along the route of the coaching inns for at least a month before she arrived. But her story was soon to take on a new dimension entirely.

The *Illustrated London News* reported:

On Tuesday, September 24th, among the visitors of the Mansion House was Mary 'Callinack', eighty-four years of age, who had travelled on foot from Penzance, carrying her few personal belongings in a basket on her back, with the object of visiting the Exhibition and of paying her respects personally to the Lord Mayor and Lady Mayoress. As soon as the ordinary business was finished the aged woman entered the justice-room, when the Lord Mayor, addressing her, said, 'Well, I understand, Mrs. Callinack, you have come to see me?"

She replied, 'Yes, God bless you. I never was in such a place before as this. I have come up asking for a small sum of money, I am, sir.' The Lord Mayor asked her where she came from and she told him, 'From Land's End, from Penzance, five weeks ago.' When she was asked why she had come to London she said, 'I had a little matter to attend to as well as to see the Exhibition. I was there yesterday, and mean to go again tomorrow. I think it very good.'

The report continued:

She then said that all her money was spent but 'five-pence-ha'penny'. After a little further conversation, which caused considerable merriment, the Lord Mayor made her a present of a sovereign, telling her to take care of it, there being a good many thieves in London. The poor creature, on receiving the gift, burst into tears and said, 'Now I will be able to get back.'

She was afterwards received by the Lady Mayoress, with whom she remained some time, and having partaken of tea in the housekeeper's room, which she said she preferred to the choicest wine in the kingdom (which latter beverage she had not tasted for sixty years), she returned thanks for the hospitality she had received and left the Mansion House.

News of Mary's visit to the Lord Mayor was quick to reach the ears of Prince Albert via a Cornishman – well connected in Royal circles – called Thomas Jago, who had been born in Bodmin. Albert gave Jago £3 to give her with his compliments and seems to have suggested that this extraordinary Cornish lady's story be brought to the attention of a sculptor – a Mr Burnard. He made sketches of her and later told the press:

She registered a vow before she left home, that she would not accept assistance in any shape, except as regarded her finances. She possesses her faculties unimpaired; is very cheerful, has a considerable amount of humour in her composition; and is withal a woman of strong common sense, and frequently makes remarks that are very shrewd, when her great age and defective education are taken into account.

The rest of Mary's story is written by Sir Theodore Martin in his *Life of the Prince Consort* and gives an account of the last day of the Great Exhibition and Mary Kelynack's part in it.

> From Windsor the Court went for some days to London for the closing of the Exhibition. 'It looked so beautiful,' she wrote in her journal, 'that I could not believe it was the last time I was to see it.' But already the dismantling had begun.
>
> The Queen refers in the next breath to a heroine of the Exhibition, an old Cornish woman named Mary 'Kerlynack', who had found the spirit to walk several hundreds of miles to behold the wonder of her generation. This day she was at one of the doors to see another sight, the Queen. 'A most hale old woman' her Majesty thought Mary, 'who was near crying at my looking at her.'

Mary returned to Cornwall, this time in some style. Now with money in her pocket and the autumn weather taking a turn for the worst, she took a series of stagecoach journeys back to Penzance. Because of the established social order of the times, she would have travelled the long and bumpy journey back to Penzance as an 'outsider' on top of the coach, along with her trusty basket of belongings. What is known for certain is that she came home from her adventures with enough memories to enthral her neighbours through the rest of her days. Here, finally, is the *Illustrated London News* again:

> She is fully aware that she has made herself somewhat famous; and among other things which she contemplates, is her return to Cornwall, to end her days in 'Paul parish,' where she wishes to be interred by the side of old Dolly Pentreath, who was also a native of Paul, and haddied at the age of 102 years.

Whether Mary Kelynack ever received the small pension that was her due is not known. She died penniless in Dock Lane, Penzance, on 5 December 1855 and was certainly buried in the same churchyard as Dolly Pentreath, which had been her greatest wish, but in an unmarked pauper's grave. It was all of 110 years earlier that John Wesley had stood on that sand bank in Newlyn and cautioned the jeering crowd about money. 'Money never stays with me', he said. 'It would burn me if it did. I throw it out of my hands as soon as possible, lest it should find its way into my heart.' Something that he and Mary Kelynack surely had in common.

'Light yourself on fire with passion and people will come from miles to watch you burn.'

A MAN ON FIRE

It was 1743 when John Wesley, the founder of Methodism, first came into Cornwall to preach, the first of thirty-one subsequent visits. Although it was a full six-day journey on horseback from London and however long or hard each day's travel had been, he always managed to find a quiet place to write up his journal by candlelight – writings that still shine a fascinating light on some of the places he visited and the people he encountered in the far West.

His preaching was directed at the poor and uneducated miners, fishermen and farm workers and their families, and happened mainly in the open air, for although he was an ordained Anglican priest, Wesley was most often denied the right to preach in the local Church of England churches by their vicars. Here he is, well on the way to Cornwall for the first time in the late summer of 1743:

Friday, 26 August
I set out for Cornwall. In the evening I preached at the cross in Taunton. A poor man had posted himself behind in order to make some disturbance: but the time was not come; the zealous wretches

who 'deny the Lord that bought them' had not yet stirred up the people. Many cried out, 'Throw down that rascal there; knock him down; beat out his brains': so that I was obliged to entreat for him more than once or he would have been but roughly handled.

Saturday, 27 August
I reached Exeter in the afternoon, but as no one knew of my coming, I did not preach that night, only to one poor sinner at the inn; who, after listening to our conversation for a while, looked earnestly at us and asked whether it was possible for one who had in some measure known 'the power of the world to come,' and was 'fallen away' (which she said was her case), to be 'renewed again to repentance.' We besought God in her behalf and left her sorrowing, yet not without hope.

Sunday, 28 August
I preached at seven to a handful of people. The sermon we heard at church was quite innocent of meaning: what that in the afternoon was, I know not; for I could not hear a single sentence. From church I went to the castle, where were gathered together (as some imagined) half the grown persons in the city. It was an awful sight. So vast a congregation in that solemn amphitheatre! And all silent and still while I explained at large and enforced that glorious truth, 'Happy are they whose iniquities are forgiven, and whose sins are covered'.

Monday, 29 August
We rode forward. About sunset we were in the middle of the first great pathless moor beyond Launceston. About eight we were got quite out of the way but we had not got far before we heard Bodmin bell. Directed by this we turned to the left and came to the town before nine.

Tuesday, 30 August
In the evening we reached St Ives. At seven I invited all guilty, helpless sinners who were conscious they 'had nothing to pay' to accept of

free forgiveness. The room was crowded both within and without but all were quiet and attentive.

Wednesday, 31 August

I spoke severally with those of the society, who were about one hundred and twenty. Nearly a hundred of these had found peace with God: such is the blessing of being persecuted for righteousness' sake! As we were going to church at eleven, a large company at the market place welcomed us with a loud huzza: wit as harmless as the ditty sung under my window (composed, one assured me, by a gentlewoman of their own town):

'John Wesley is come to town,
To try if he can pull the churches down'.

In the evening I explained 'the promise of the Father.' After preaching, many began to be turbulent; but John Nelson went into the midst of them, spoke a little to the loudest, who answered not again but went quietly away.

Saturday, 3 September

I rode to the Three-cornered Down (so called), nine or ten miles east of St Ives, where we found two or three hundred tinners, who had been some time waiting for us. They all appeared quite pleased and unconcerned and many of them ran after us to Gwennap (two miles east), where their number was quickly increased to four or five hundred. I had much comfort here in applying these words, 'He hath anointed me to preach the gospel to the poor'. One who lived near invited us to lodge at his house and conducted us back to the Green in the morning. We came thither just as the day dawned. At Trezuthan Downs, five miles nearer St Ives, we found seven or eight hundred people, to whom I cried aloud, 'Cast away all your transgressions; for why will ye die, O house of Israel?' After dinner I preached again to about a thousand people. It was here first I observed a little impression made on two or three of the hearers; the rest, as usual, showing huge approbation and absolute unconcern.

Friday, 9 September

I rode in quest of St Hilary downs, ten or twelve miles south east of St Ives. And the Downs I found, but no congregation – neither man, woman, nor child. But by that I had put on my gown and cassock, about a hundred gathered themselves together, whom I earnestly called 'to repent and believe the gospel.' And if but one heard, it was worth all the labour.

Saturday, 10 September

There were prayers at St Just in the afternoon, which did not end till four. I then preached at the Cross to, I believe, a thousand people, who all behaved in a quiet and serious manner. At six I preached at Sennan[*sic*], near the Land's End; and appointed the little congregation (consisting chiefly of old, grey-headed men) to meet me again at five in the morning. But on Sunday, 11, a great part of them were got together between three and four o'clock: so between four and five we began praising God. We went afterwards down, as far as we could go safely, toward the point of the rocks at the Land's End. It was an awful sight! But how will these melt away when God shall arise to judgment! The sea between does indeed 'boil like a pot.' Between eight and nine I preached at St Just, on the green plain near the town, to the largest congregation (I was informed) that ever had been seen in these parts.

Monday, 12 September found him in the Scilly Isles:

I had had for some time a great desire to go and publish the love of God our Saviour, if it were but for one day, in the Isles of Scilly; and I had occasionally mentioned it to several. This evening three of our brethren came and offered to carry me thither if I could procure the mayor's boat, which, they said, was the best sailer of any in the town. I sent, and he lent it me immediately. So the next morning, John Nelson, Mr. Shepherd, and I, with three men and a pilot, sailed from St Ives. It seemed strange to me to attempt going in a fisher-boat, fifteen leagues upon the main ocean, especially when the waves began to swell and hang over our heads. But I called to my companions, and we joined together in singing lustily and with a good courage. About half an hour after one, we landed on St Mary's, the chief of the inhabited islands.

We immediately waited upon the Governor, with the usual present, namely, a newspaper. I desired him, likewise, to accept of an 'Earnest Appeal.' The minister not being willing I should preach in the church, I preached, at six, in the streets to almost all the town and many soldiers, sailors, and workmen. It was a blessed time so that I scarcely knew how to conclude. After the sermon I gave them some little books and hymns, which they were so eager to receive that they were ready to tear both them and me to pieces.

For what political reason such a number of workmen were gathered together and employed at so large an expense to fortify a few barren rocks, which whosoever would take, deserves to have them for his pains, I could not possibly devise: but a providential reason was easy to be discovered. God might call them together to hear the gospel, which perhaps otherwise they might never have thought of.

At five in the morning I preached again and between nine and ten, having talked with many in private and distributed both to them and others between two and three hundred hymns and little books, we left this barren, dreary place and set sail for St Ives, though the wind was strong and blew directly in our teeth. Our pilot said we should have good luck if we reached the land; but he knew not Him whom the winds and seas obey. Soon after three we were even with the Land's End, and about nine we reached St Ives.

Perhaps the most remarkable of his sermons on that first visit was preached at an extraordinary place – today sensitively 'remodelled' and much visited. It is a grass-lined amphitheatre called Gwennap Pit, some 2½ miles from Redruth:

Tuesday, 20 September
At Trezuthan Downs I preached to two or three thousand people on the 'highway' of the Lord, the way of holiness. We reached Gwennap a little before six and found the plain covered from end to end. It was

supposed there were ten thousand people, to whom I preached. I could not conclude till it was so dark we could scarcely see one another. And there was on all sides the deepest attention; none speaking, stirring, or scarcely looking aside. Surely here, though in a temple not made with hands, was God worshipped in 'the beauty of holiness'. [He preached at that remarkable place a further eighteen times over the years.]

Wednesday, 21 September
I was awakened between three and four by a large company of tinners who, fearing they should be too late, had gathered round the house and were singing and praising God. At five I preached once more. They all devoured the Word. Oh, may it be health to their soul and marrow unto their bones! We rode to Launceston that day.

Thursday, 22 September
As we were riding through a village called Sticklepath, one stopped me in the street and asked abruptly, 'Is not thy name John Wesley?' Immediately two or three more came up and told me I must stop there. I did so; and before we had spoken many words, our souls took acquaintance with each other. I found they were called Quakers: but that hurt not me, seeing the love of God was in their hearts.

John Wesley died in 1791, aged 88. Six years before the end, he wrote in his journal:

It is now eleven years since I have felt any such thing as weariness; many times I speak till my voice fails, and I can speak no longer. Frequently I walk till my strength fails, and I can walk no farther; yet even then I feel no sensation of weariness but am perfectly easy from head to foot. I dare not impute this to natural causes: it is the will of God.

During his long life Wesley travelled 250,000 miles on horseback, preached over 30,000 sermons – described as 'doctrinal, not dogmatic' – wrote and edited some 400 publications, and believed in a personal salvation and that it was crucial to 'love your neighbour as you love yourself'. The last time he preached in Cornwall was at Gwennap Pit again, where he left the tens of thousands who had come to listen to him with this memorable advice, perhaps inspired by his memory of the Aesop's fable of the grasshopper who fiddled away the summer while the ant worked hard to put in stores for the winter. He told them, 'Earn all you can, save all you can, give all you can.'

Wesley's legacy to the county is that today the Cornwall Methodist District covers almost all of Cornwall and the Isles of Scilly and totals some 257 churches.

He was a great man – a giant in the field of mechanical invention, a born genius whose extraordinary powers enabled him to move far ahead of his times.

SINGING TREVITHICK'S PRAISES

The Cornish have an anthem they roar out from the terraces at Twickenham during rugby matches. It is in praise of the great Cornish engineer Richard Trevithick, who on Christmas Eve 1801 drove a steam-powered road engine up (and then down) Camborne Hill: hence the chorus, invariably delivered with wild, pantomime gestures:

Goin' up Camborne Hill, coming down
Goin' up Camborne Hill, coming down
The horses stood still;
The wheels went around;
Going up Camborne Hill coming down.

In 1801 Robert Trevithick was 30 years of age, 6ft 3in tall, built like an ox, was an accomplished wrestler and would have made a great prop forward for Cornwall except that he had a temper and it would be a further twenty years before someone picked up a ball at Rugby School and ran with it. But neither Trevithick's means nor education would have got him into Rugby. He was born in the Illogan district of Cornwall in 1771, one of a family of five, of whom Richard was the only surviving son, and therefore very much his mother's pride and joy. He went to the little school in Camborne where he was described as 'disobedient, slow, lazy, inattentive, and obstinate, always drawing upon his slate lines and figures, unintelligible to any but himself'. His own father, a manager at the local tin mine, thought him a loafer, and Richard remained semi-literate throughout his career, although he had a gift for calculations and was always an extremely practical youth: those 'unintelligible drawings' perhaps contained the germs of those inventions that would one day contribute hugely to the success of Cornish mining, and make his name famous around the world.

The large boy grew into a large man, noted especially for his feats of strength. He could easily lift his own weight in iron and was famed for throwing the sledgehammer an enormous distance over an engine house, purely for the fun of it. But Richard Trevithick was endowed with more than physical strength; having first received some instruction in his calling from a well-known Cornish engineer called Bull. This was in 1790; he was just 19 and he began to work at Stray Park Mine at £1.50 a month. Because of his intuitive ability to solve problems that perplexed educated engineers, he was selected to report upon the relative merits of Watt's and Hornblower's engines, which were being used as pumps and to power lifting gear in other rival mines. They employed low-pressure steam because high pressures were considered too dangerous. But Trevithick thought differently and said that by using high-pressure steam and allowing it to expand within the cylinder, the same amount of power could be produced in a smaller and lighter engine. He used these engines to drive iron-rolling mills and even propel a barge using paddle wheels.

He had married Jane Harvey of Hayle in 1797 and they lived first in Redruth and then Camborne, and it was here, in their home, where the idea for a road vehicle first took shape. It stemmed from his having to transport one of his portable engines from mine to mine – an expensive and labour-intensive process – and it was discussed one evening around the supper table in the Trevithick parlour. Here the assembled company was confronted by an actual working model, which was put on the table in front of them. 'Why not, with all this available power, make the engine move herself?' Trevithick asked. Significantly, the guests included Davies

Gilbert, later to become president of the Royal Society, who acted as stoker, and Lady Frances de Dunstanville of Tehidy (on whose husband's estates most of the great Camborne mines were situated), playing the part of engine-man to a little model locomotive that then ran noisily around the table, emitting clouds of smoke and puffing steam.

Came Christmas Eve, 1801 the full-size Puffing Devil made its first public appearance on the roads round Camborne, Tuckingmill and Tehidy, towing a truck with ten passengers up Camborne Hill – 'faster than a man could walk' – and then down again. The success, though not complete, was sufficient to determine Trevithick, with his brother-in-law, Andrew Vivian – who found the money and shared in the speculation – to head for London in order to obtain a patent, the first of many. It was on this trip that they were set upon by a band of pickpockets. Trevithick seized two of them and knocked their heads together before picking them up bodily and throwing each of them in opposite directions.

A second engine was built and exhibited to the public, first at Lord's Cricket Ground and afterwards near the spot that would one day become the headquarters of the London and North Western Railway, at Euston. That engine got up such a head of steam that it reached a speed of 12mph. It later hurtled along Oxford Street, where all horses and carriages had been ordered out of the way and many of the shops shut for fear of accidents, while the roofs of the houses were crowded with spectators.

He also went on to exhibit his newer 'Catch-me-who-can' engine, on a circular railway of about 100ft in diameter built in Hyde Park. It drew great crowds of Londoners at 1s per head to witness the extraordinary novelty. But the admission fees did not come in fast enough to offset the legal difficulties he had to contend with in the working of the ill-defined patent laws. The final straw came when the wrought-iron railway track gave way and the engine overturned.

Trevithick, a quick-tempered and impulsive man, was entirely lacking in business sense. A later untrustworthy business partner caused the failure of the London business he had started in 1808 for the manufacture of a type of iron tank Trevithick had patented. Ill health, in the form of first typhus, then gastric and subsequently brain fevers, took their toll; bankruptcy and debtors' prison followed and his eventual freedom came at a price as he sold one of his patents to a competitor.

Jane Trevithick and her four young children joined him in London and found him in a sorry state. The last two letters she had written to him she found unopened and unread in his jacket pocket – tucked away, she believed, because he had been too immersed in his work to read them. The truth however, he told her through his tears, was 'that they might contain your argument against our reunion'. It was as well for both that his faithful wife had come to town when she did. Poor Trevithick was at a low ebb and, after two and more years living and working in Limehouse on various engineering projects, was eventually driven from London after his unsuccessful application had been made to the government for remuneration for his truly national services.

He returned to Cornwall, where his versatility in his profession seems to have revived his spirit and drove him on to new challenges and inventions. Had he possessed the financial acumen to go with his engineering brilliance, this period in his life would have made him a fortune. In 1813 he oversaw Plymouth Breakwater, before turning his attention to the manufacture of agricultural engines, the first steam thrashing machine, the new 'pole-puffer-engine' and a whole string of patented pumps and other steam-driven machinery to serve mining and industry in many parts of the country.

But 20 October 1816 found him outward bound for darkest Peru, by invitation of the owners of the new silver mines. These deep pits were at high altitude above sea level so that their atmospheric pumps could not lift water from the ever-deepening mines. Trevithick's exploits, successes and especially setbacks and failures in South America were many and sometimes dramatic – including being forced to join the army of Simon Bolivar during the revolution, living off a diet of fruit and monkeys in Chile, and once being very nearly eaten by an alligator. He finally borrowed money for this boat fare home and limped back to Falmouth on 9 October 1827, eleven years after he had set out 'to discover El Dorado'.

He returned with the clothes he stood up in, a gold watch, a pair of dividers, a pocket compass and a pair of spurs. But he had the happiness of finding his wife and their family of four sons and two daughters all well and waiting for him at Camborne, where the church bells rang out in his honour and he was entertained at the houses of all the principal people in the county. Poor Jane had remained loyal to him during those long years of financial difficulty and separation. He had thought that she would be receiving regular income from the revenue generated by his many patents but he was wrong. She had received no money from him during his South American sojourn and none from the patents he had thought to be protecting his ideas and generating a small fortune. Alas, most of them had been altered in subtle ways and exported by competitors. During his absence, Jane and the children had been supported entirely by her brother, Henry Harvey.

Trevithick was now 59 years of age and found that he had to begin life anew. He managed to secure £1,000 from one mine that had benefitted from his inventions but no other. His inventive genius but poor head for business continued, and so too did his ill health.

One of his last projects was designed as an entry in a government competition to devise something spectacular to commemorate the recently passed Reform Bill of 1832. His creative genius came up with the plan to build a perforated, gilt-coated, cast-iron column, 1,000ft high, to be erected in the heart of London near to St Paul's. For comparison, Nelson's Column, completed in 1840, is 169ft 3in or 51.59m high. One of many novel features in Trevithick's planned column was the 'air-elevator', which would be in a tube in the centre of the column and shoot twenty-five Georgian thrill-seekers from the base to the summit at some speed, at which point they would exit the car at the viewing platform for a breathtaking view of the capital. The scheme seems also to have taken the judges' breath away, for nothing came of his submission.

But the end was approaching. Trevithick had been in poor health when he died, on 22 April 1833, at his lodgings in the Bull Hotel in Dartford, Kent: 'a demise that was probably accelerated by poverty and misery'. He had been working at Hall's Engineering Works at Dartford and his family and friends in Cornwall had known nothing of his illness. He was penniless and was indebted to charity for his grave, and to the mechanics at the factory for becoming the bearers and the only mourners at his simple funeral. Jane Trevithick lived to the age of 96. She died at Pencliffe, Hayle, in 1868. Of their six children, Francis Trevithick (1812–77) became chief mechanical engineer of the London and North Western Railway.

Richard Trevithick was an engineering genius and his too short career enlightened the era's great Industrial Revolution, promoting Cornwall's technical prowess around the world. It is not only rugby crowds that honour his memory: the good people of Camborne celebrate Trevithick Day each year as a community-led street festival of free entertainment, always held on the last Saturday of April – that month being both the day of his birth and of his passing – when the Trevithick Society wheel out their reproduction 'Puffing Devil', fire it up and take it, 'faster than a man can walk', 'Goin' up Camborne Hill, coming down!'

EDWARD JOHN TRELAWNY
From a sketch by Seymour Kirkup

*He outlived the other Romantics of his era and went on to shock the next
generation of straight-laced Victorians.*

NEVER 'LORD BYRON'S JACKAL'

He told the world he was born in Cornwall and certainly came from an
old Cornish family of that name, sharing it with Sir John Trelawny of
Pelynt – he of 'The Song of the Western Men' fame. But he was born with
a wanderlust that drove him throughout his long and adventure-filled
life. He was the author and adventurer Edward John Trelawny (1792–
1881), a handsome, dashing and quixotic individual who cultivated the
friendships of some of the Romantic era's greatest literary figures.

Contemporaries dismissed him as a hanger-on to figures such as the
critic, essayist and poet, Leigh Hunt and the poets Shelley and Byron
– especially to Byron and he was dubbed by a jealous society as 'Lord
Byron's jackal' when he sought them out in Switzerland and then Italy,
in 1822. Shelley's wife, Mary, author of *Frankenstein*, was overwhelmed
by the handsome raconteur. 'He is extravagant,' she confided to her diary,
'and has the rare merit of exciting my imagination.' Then later, 'He is
clever; for his moral qualities I am yet in the dark; he is a strange web
which I am endeavouring to unravel.'

Having been a young midshipman in an earlier life, he taught Shelley to sail and when the poet was later drowned off Viareggio in a storm, Trelawny arranged the funeral pyre on the beach where the body was burned. While Leigh Hunt denied Byron (mad, bad and dangerous to know) his request to take Shelley's skull away with him – to turn into a macabre drinking cup, he later wrote – Trelawney is said to have reached into the embers and retrieved the poet's heart, for Mary: which spontaneous gesture made him famous with his readers in later years.

At the outbreak of the war for Greek independence, Trelawny and Byron left for Greece, where Trelawney immediately joined the fighting under the rebel leader Odysseus Androutsos and married his half-sister, Tersitsa. In fact, he was married four times, once to a 13-year old girl. Unsurprisingly, none of the marriages lasted very long and he also had a string of mistresses between times, eventually dying quietly in his sleep in Surrey at the age of 88.

But no account of Trelawney's wildly chequered career would be complete without mention of his journey to America in 1833. There he met the famous English actress Fanny Kemble. They visited Niagara Falls together where, on a whim, he stepped out of his clothes and attempted to swim across the Niagara River between the rapids and the falls. Later that year, in Charleston, South Carolina, he paid £1,000 for a black slave (the bill of sale still exists) and sent him to Canada via the so-called Underground Railroad escape route, something he had done for other slaves on other occasions in both Asia and in Greece.

Little wonder that this swashbuckling Cornishman, adventurer and poet won so many admirers during the increasingly straight-laced Victorian era. Swinburne, the poet who called him 'a magnificent old Viking to look at', also wrote, 'There is some fresh air in England yet while such an Englishman is alive!' Although he died in England, his ashes are buried in the Protestant Cemetery in Rome, alongside Shelley. Mary Shelley kept the heart Trelawny had rescued for her in a silken shroud. In 1852, a year after she died, the heart was found in her desk, wrapped in the pages of one of her late husband's last poems, 'Adonais'. It was eventually buried in the family vault with their son, in St Peter's Church, Bournemouth.

Cornwall's forgotten heroine.

'THAT BLOODY WOMAN!'

In distant South Africa, 8,300 miles from St Ive where she was born, Emily Hobhouse is famous for being the woman who saved the lives of countless numbers of women and children in the concentration camps created by Britain during the Boer War (1899–1902) and her name is still revered there as 'the Angel of Love'.

Yet in Britain, she is still more often known as 'Cornwall's forgotten heroine' for there were many of her countrymen at that time who painted her as a traitor to the Empire, aiding and assisting the enemy when British troops were engaged in a hit-and-run war with Dutch settlers, the Afrikaners. Kitchener himself referred to her as 'that bloody woman' and when she died in 1926 after a lifetime spent serving humanity in both the Boer and Great War, no Cornish newspaper so much as recorded her passing.

This extraordinary woman, born in 1860 in east Cornwall at St Ive – pronounced 'eve' and not to be confused with St Ives – was the youngest daughter of six children. Her father was Reginald Hobhouse, the local vicar and after her mother's death Emily spent the next fourteen or so years looking after him. Her upbringing was very Victorian and she had no formal education but had well-connected relatives in London, through whom she made several 'political connections'. Her father died in 1895, leaving each of his children a legacy of several thousand pounds.

She was 35 and was now able to put into plan an idea she had nursed for several years. She sailed for America and headed to Massachusetts and a wide-open 'wild west' town called Virginia. It was in the middle of a forest, and although barely four years old, it had already burned down once and its wooden buildings, flanking each side of a single street, were home to some forty-seven saloons, several hundred 'saloon girls' and 4,000 Cornish miners away from home.

Emily spent her time there doing good works. She founded a Sunday school, a library, tended the sick and injured, spread the word of temperance, became an active member of the church – and fell in love with a handsome man who turned out to be 'a bad lot'. His name was John Carr Jackson, an ambitious man especially attracted to her money. They became engaged and she was persuaded to buy a ranch in Mexico, which was a financial disaster. The marriage never took place and she returned to England in 1898, broken-hearted and penniless. In her luggage was her wedding veil, which she thenceforward carried with her always.

A year later, at the outbreak of the Second Boer War, she was approached by a Liberal MP in London, who asked her to become secretary of the women's branch of the South African Conciliation Committee, of which he was president. She travelled to South Africa in 1900 to find out about the plight of the Boer women and children at first hand. What she found appalled her. Britain had built concentration camps in South Africa to house them – these were not extermination camps of the kind Hitler would build in the Second World War – they were established by the British as part of their military campaign against two small Afrikaner republics: the ZAR (Transvaal) and the Orange Free State.

After Lord Roberts, Chief Commander of the British forces, occupied the Free State capital, Bloemfontein, on 13 March 1900, he issued a proclamation inviting the Boers to lay down their arms and sign an oath of neutrality. They would then be free to return to their farms on the understanding that they would no longer participate in the war.

Eventually, around 20,000 Boers – about a third – made use of this offer. They were called the 'protected burghers'. Roberts had banked on this policy to end the war. But after the British occupation of the Transvaal capital, Pretoria, on 5 June 1900, there was no end in sight. On the contrary, the Boers had started a guerrilla war, which included attacks on railway lines.

In reaction, Roberts ordered that for every attack on a railway line the closest homestead would be burnt down. This was the start of the scorched earth policy. When this did not work, homesteads were burnt in a radius of 16km, all livestock killed or taken and all crops destroyed.

When Lord Kitchener took over from Roberts as commander in November 1900, homesteads and whole towns were burnt down, even if there was no attack on any railway. In this way almost all Boer homesteads – about 30,000 in all – were razed to the ground and thousands of livestock killed. The two republics were entirely devastated.

But the scorched earth policy had led to more and more Boer women and children being left homeless. Roberts decided to bring them into the camps, too. They were called the 'undesirables' – families of Boers who were still 'on commando' or already prisoners of war. They were given fewer rations than others in the camps. Over 100,000 black people were also forced into the camps. Emily was shocked at the terrible conditions she found and believed that if people in Britain knew about them then something would be done to change things. She wrote about them for the *Guardian* newspaper and sent an official report to the British Government.

On her return to Britain she was treated harshly by the authorities and newspapers, especially *The Times*. She was accused of threatening Britain's war effort. Lord Kitchener only ever referred to her as 'that bloody woman' but eventually the government set up its own investigation into conditions. She had written:

> Crass male ignorance, helplessness and muddling … I rub as much salt into the sore places in their minds … because it is good for them; but I can't help melting a little when they are very humble and confess that the whole thing is a grievous and gigantic blunder and presents almost insoluble problems, and they don't know how to face.

She tried to return to South Africa in 1901 but was not allowed to enter the country and was literally frog-marched back up the gangplank of the ship that had brought her. However, she did return several times after the war to continue helping the Boer women and children. She also publicly opposed the First World War, asking for peace.

In later life Emily was made an Honorary Citizen of South Africa. Money was raised for her by the Boer people, which she used to buy a house in St Ives, Cornwall. She died, alone, in London in 1926, aged 66 but her ashes are buried at the National Women's Monument, Bloemfontein, erected to commemorate the death and suffering of 26,000 women and children. No Cornish newspaper then chose to report her death but there is a memorial to her now in St Ive Parish Church, Callington.

Whether the weather be cold, or whether the weather be hot,
We'll weather the weather, whatever the weather,
Whether we like it or not.

CORNISH WEATHER LORE

They get a lot of weather in Cornwall and over many hundreds of years they have had plenty of useful things to say on the subject. 'Lore', of course, is knowledge that has been accumulated over time through education or experience, so what follows is probably still worth mulling over in this day and age, before planning a picnic, say, or renting a boat.

Back in 1703, when every Cornishman needed to be his own weather forecaster, the peninsula experienced what meteorologists today call an extratropical cyclone. It hit the South West hard and blew for six days and nights at the end of November and the beginning of December of that year. The deaths of more than 8,000 people and the catastrophic destruction it caused had no equal in recorded memory and was chronicled by Daniel Defoe in his book *The Storm*. He wrote: 'No pen could describe it, nor tongue express it, nor thought conceive it unless by one in the extremity of it.'

In London alone, 2,000 massive chimney stacks were blown down; the lead roof was torn from Westminster Abbey, Queen Anne was forced to shelter in a cellar and, on the Thames, some 700 ships were blown into a single heap in the Pool of London. There was great flooding in the West Country, where 400 windmills were destroyed, some with the wind driving their wooden gears so fast that they burst into flames. Hundreds of people drowned in flooding on the Somerset Levels, thousands of sheep and cattle were drowned and a ship was found 15 miles (24km) inland.

The first Eddystone Lighthouse off Plymouth and 9 miles (14km) south of Cornwall's Rame Head was totally destroyed on 27 November, killing all six occupants, including its builder, Henry Winstanley. A ship was torn from its moorings in the Helford River in Cornwall and was blown for 200 miles (320km) on bare masts before grounding eight hours later on the Isle of Wight.

Unhelpfully perhaps, the Church of England declared it to be 'a punishment brought by God for the sins of the nation'. Is it little wonder, therefore, that Cornwall especially has so much folklore attached to forecasting its weather?

JANUARY

Ancient Cornish name: Mis-jenver, cold air month.

> If Janiveer calends be summerly gay,
> 'Twill be wintry weather till the calends of May.
>
> A snow year, a rich year.
> The blackest month of all the year
> Is the month of Janiveer.
> If the grass grow in Janiveer
> 'Twill be the worse for 't all the year.
>
> Under water famine, under snow bread.
>
> March in Janiveer? Janiveer in March I fear.

FEBRUARY

Ancient Cornish name: Hu-evral, whirling month.

Candlemas shined, and the winter's behind. [2 February]

If Candlemas Day be fair and bright
The winter will take another flight;
But if it should be dark and drear
Then winter is gone for another year.

When the wind's in the East on Candlemas Day,
There it will stick till the second of May.

MARCH

Ancient Cornish name: Miz-merp, horse month.

Upon St David's Day [1 March] put oats and barley in the clay.

If it does not freeze on the 10th of March a fertile year may be expected.

In March and in April, from morning to night,
In sowing and setting good huswives delight:
To have in a garden or other like plot,
To trim up their house, and to furnish their pot.

Thunder in spring, cold will bring.

Spring is here when you can tread on nine
daisies at once on the village green.

In spring a tub of rain makes a spoonful of mud.
In autumn a spoonful of rain makes a tub of mud.

APRIL

Ancient Cornish name: Miz-ebrall, primrose month.

> If it thunders on All Fool's day
> It brings good crops of grain and hay.
> The first thunder of the year awakes
> All the frogs and all the snakes.

Parsley sown on Good Friday bears a heavier crop than that sown on any other day. Parsley seed goes nine times to the Devil before coming up. It only comes up partially because the Devil takes his tithe of it.

There is an old superstition that where one hears the cuckoo first there one will spend most of the year.

A cold April, the barn will fill.

When there are many more swifts than swallows in the spring, expect a hot and dry summer.

MAY

Ancient Cornish name: Miz-me, flowery month.

Lo, the young month comes, all smiling, up this way.
A windy May makes a fair year.

The fair maid, who, the first of May,
Goes to the fields at break of day,
And washes in dew from the hawthorn tree,
Will ever after handsome be.

Go and look at oats in May,
You will see them blown away;

Go and look again in June,
You will sing another tune.

Cut thistles in May,
They grow in a day;
Cut thistles in June,
That is too soon;
Cut thistles in July,
Then they will die.

JUNE

Ancient Cornish name: Miz-epham, summer month, or head of summer.

If it raineth on the eighth of June a wet harvest men will see.

A calm June, puts the farmer in tune.
A dripping June, puts all things in tune.

Pondweed sinks before rain. Fir cones close for wet, open for fine weather.

If nights three dewless there be,
'Twill rain you're sure to see.

If bees stay at home
Rain will soon come.
If they fly away
Fine will be the day.

When the wind veers against the sun, trust it not, for back 'twill run.

Rainbow to windward, foul falls the day; rainbow to leeward, damp runs away. A rainbow at morn, put your hook in the corn; a rainbow at eve, put your head in the sheave.

A fog and a small moon bring an easterly wind soon.

JULY

Ancient Cornish name: Miz-gorepham, head of the summer month.

If the first of July be rainy weather, 't will rain more or less for four weeks together.

The nightingale and the cuckow both grow hoarse at the rising of Sirius the dogge star.

St Swithun doth christen the apples. [15 July]

No tempest good July, Lest the corn look ruely.

While wormwood hath seed, get a handful or twain,
To save against March, to make flea to refrain:
Where chamber is sweepid, and wormwood is strown,
No flea for his life, dare abide to be known.

If St Swithin's Day brings rain it will rain for forty days, but if fair, forty days of fair weather follow.

AUGUST

Ancient Cornish name: Miz-east, harvest month.

Loaf-mass Day (1 August). A day of offering first fruits, when a loaf was given to the priests in place of the first fruits.

St James's Day. Oyster Day (5 August)

Who eats oysters on St James's Day will never want.

It is always windy in barley harvests; it blows off the heads for the poor.

On Thursday at three, look out and you'll see, what Friday will be.

For morning rain leave not your journey.

To smell wild thyme will renew spirits and energy in long walks under an August sun.

Friday's a day as'll have his trick, the fairest or foulest day o' the wick.

St Bartholomew's Day (24 August)

If St Bartholomew's Day be misty, the morning beginning with a hoar frost, then cold weather will soon ensue, and a sharp winter attended with many biting frosts.

SEPTEMBER

Ancient Cornish name: Miz-guerda gala, white straw month.

September blow soft, till the fruit's in the loft.

A bloom upon the apple tree when the apples are ripe's a sure termination to somebody's life.

September fifteenth is said to be fine in six years out of seven.

Onion skin very thin, mild winter coming in; onion skin thick and tough, coming winter cold and rough.

St Matthew's Day (21 September)

St Matthee shut up the bee.

If Michaelmas Day [29 September] be fair, the sun will shine much in the winter; though the wind at northeast will frequently reign long, and be very sharp and nipping.

The Michaelmas moon rises nine nights alike soon.

If you eat goose on Michaelmas Day you will never want money all the year round.

OCTOBER

Ancient Cornish name: Miz-hedra, watery month.

St Francis and St Benedight died 4 October 1226.

> St Francis and St Benedight,
> Blesse this house from wicked wight
> From the night-mare, and the goblin
> That is night Good-Fellow-Robin;
> Keep it from all evil spirits,
> Fairies, weezils, rats, and ferrets:
> From curfew time,
> To the next prime.

> Who soweth in rain
> Hath weed to his pain;
> But worse shall he speed
> That soweth ill seed.

Full moon in October without frost, no frost till full moon in November.

Hoar frost and gipsies never stay nine days in a place.

There are always nineteen fine days in October.

NOVEMBER

Ancient Cornish name: Miz-dui, black month.

All Saints' Day (1 November).

> Who sets an apple tree may live to see it end,
> Who sets a pear tree may set it for a friend.

> An early winter, a surly winter.

St Martin's Day (11 November)

> If Martinmas ice can bear a duck,
> The winter will be all mire and muck.

> 'Tween Martinmas and Yule,
> Water's wine in every pool.

> If it is cold, fair, and dry at Martinmas, the cold in winter will not last long.

St Edmund's Day (20 November)

> Set garlike and pease, St Edmund to please.

> If on Friday it rain,
> 'Twill on Sunday again;
> If Friday be clear,
> Have for Sunday no fear.

> From twelve to two
> See what the day will do.

DECEMBER

Ancient Cornish name: Miz-kavardine, following black month.

> December frost and January flood
> Never boded husbandman good.

> When there are three days cold, expect three days colder.

St Thomas's Day (21 December)

> St Thomas grey St Thomas grey,
> The longest night and the shortest day.

> Look at the weathercock on St Thomas's Day at twelve o'clock, and see
> which way the wind is, and there it will stick for the next three months

> If Christmas Day on Monday be,
> A great winter that year you'll see.
> If that Christmas Day should fall
> Upon Friday, know well all
> That winter season shall be easy,
> Save great winds aloft shall fly.

St Stephen's Day (26 December)

Innocents' Day, or Childermas Day (28 December)

> 'T is unlucky to begin any work on Childermas Day, and what soever day
> that falls on, whether on the Monday, or Tuesday, or any other, nothing
> must be begun on that day through the year.

So, what to do if you missed the weather forecast this morning, have taken all of this in and don't believe a word of it? Then do what any wise Cornish weather-watcher has been doing for hundreds of years and open and close a drawer or a door, or a wooden framed window.

If they'm stick, rain's on the way. But when dew's on the grass, rain'll never come to pass.

As some sez in Mowsel – and simla such places – 'Lowena dhis!' [Have a nice day!]

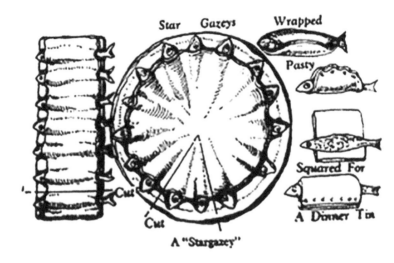

Star Gazeys Wrapped

Pasty

Squared For

A Dinner Tin

A "Stargazey"

A merry plaas you may believe
woz Mowsel pon Tom Bawcock's Eve.
To be theer then oo wudn wesh
To sup o sibm soorts o fesh!

SEA WATCHING AND STARGAZING

Once upon a time pilchards were plentiful round the Cornish peninsula. In the first half of the eighteenth century the total number salted, packed into barrels and shipped from Cornish ports averaged 30,000 hogsheads annually, a total of 900 million fish.

Every coastal community had lookouts to watch for the great shoals and alert the fishermen by shouting 'Heva, heva!', which in old Cornish means 'swarming' or 'flocking'. In those times it was thought unlucky to eat pilchards, or any kind of fish, from the head downwards because it would be 'sure to turn the heads of the fish away from the coasts'. On the other hand, eating the fish from the tail towards the head brought the fish into shore and good luck to the fishermen.

Most of the catch in those days, strangely enough, went to Italy but sufficient stayed at home to feed the fishermen and their families. When prolonged storms kept the boats in harbour, people grew hungry and in bad years the situation could become desperate. Enter Mousehole's legendary fisherman, Tom Bawcock. The old man made a name for himself one Christmas time some two centuries earlier when he saved the day by daring to put out to sea in a great storm that had kept everyone else's boats in harbour for weeks.

He returned with his small boat loaded up to the gunnels with fish – seven kinds of fish to be precise – and a great pie was baked in his honour, a so-called 'Stargazey' pie of fish, eggs and boiled potatoes. To this day the pie is baked and served with the heads of the fish poking out of the pastry to show off Tom's endeavour in lifting the famine, and Mousehole makes a ceremony of it on 23 December each year.

The seven fish the original pie contained probably included sand eels, mackerel, herring, dogfish, ling and, of course, pilchards, but nowadays any white fish will do – plus pilchards for the fun of it, of course.

Not all tails are what they might appear at first glance.

THE UNVARNISHED TRUTH ABOUT MERMAIDS

Mermaids spell bad news, especially for gullible seafaring men away from home: always have. But that should not stop holiday visitors keeping their eyes peeled for one, especially around our estuaries – their most likely hangout – and making themselves inconspicuous by sunning themselves on sandbanks between the seals.

Millions of matelots have been tempted with siren song and lured by womanly wiles until they come to sticky ends, sometimes on estuary sandbanks but usually on the rocks. It is why so many waterside inns were called 'The Mermaid' and how, since medieval times, the word became a euphemism for … well, let's say a tavern wench.

After the Armada sailed past our Western shores on its fateful voyage to stormy destruction, the Elizabethan propaganda machine was quick to commission *The Armada Portrait* of the queen. With the hurricane-tossed Spanish ships at the top of the picture and a brazen mermaid to Elizabeth's left (Latin, *sinister*) side, the message was clear: she not only controlled the elements, she could also summon seamen-savaging sirens. So Spanish sailor, beware.

Quite how mermaids leave the water and travel overland has never been fully explained in Cornwall – where they seem to flourish – but in the church of St Senara in the village of Zennor in west Cornwall is a carving of a mermaid who did just that. She is depicted with flowing hair, a mirror in one hand and a comb in the other, and there is a strange story about her.

She visited the church several times, locals will tell you, a beautiful and richly dressed lady with a glorious singing voice. Came the Sunday that a handsome young chorister called Mathey Trewella followed her as she walked away towards the cliffs. She had fallen in love with his singing and neither Mathey nor the mermaid were ever seen again. The villagers hurriedly carved the mermaid as a warning to other young men against the wiles of the merrymaids, as they are still called in those parts.

While our shores today can boast a Mermaid's Cove in north Devon, the picture postcard fishing village of Clovelly can provide the best credentials for luring mermaid spotters to its steep street, for this is the very place that inspired the Victorian fairy story of *The Water Babies*. Charles Kingsley was an Anglican minister, a devout Christian and a social reformer, and his narrative is a highly moral tale. It is a parable that has not stood the test of time and the original makes for some fairly uncomfortable reading nowadays. Little Tom, the chimney sweep hero of the book, is drowned as he attempts to flee his harsh world of slavery and his cruel master, Grimes – this while in the throes of washing away his coating of black soot in a stream. But wait, he is reborn and lives and grows in a magical, fairy world beneath the waves.

Kingsley, aged 11, almost certainly knew a Tom, a fisherman's son, among his playmates when he came to live at Clovelly in 1831, where his father became rector. Storms along that unsheltered coast were many and often took lives, and one of these is reported in the *Exeter Flying Post*:

> About sixty boats, employed in the herring fishery at Clovelly, were, on Thursday evening, by the suddenness of a gale of wind, obliged to relinquish their nets in the hopes of gaining the shore in safety, but unfortunately more than forty were driven among the rocks. The cries of the drowning, thirty-five in number, most of whom have left large families, produced an effect too heart rending to be adequately expressed.

The body of one small boy was found on the shore the next day, still tied to the broken mast of his father's upturned boat. Tom perhaps? Although it would not be until 1862 that he wrote his story of 'fairies and mermaids' and their many adventures under the sea, Kingsley never forgot Clovelly and the lot of the poor fishermen there.

So, do mermaids exist? Darwin had published his *Origins of Species* in 1859 and Kingsley, a friend and admirer, defended it vigorously after his own book had been called 'total nonsense' by those who chose to dismiss it in its entirety because of its social significance.

Kingsley was probably smiling when he retaliated with, 'No person is qualified to say that something that they have never seen (like a human soul or a water baby) does not exist till they have seen no water babies existing, which is quite a different thing, mind, from not seeing water babies'. So there's an end to it.